Fundamentals of Real Time Distributed Simulation

By

John Nicol

About The Author

John Nicol has been involved in the Modeling and Simulation industry for over 20 years. A retired Major serving with the New Zealand Army, postings included the New Zealand Army Simulation Center and various command and training roles. After leaving the military John has been involved in strategic M&S programs and contracts for the Canadian Forces (CF), including Project Manager with the CF Synthetic Environment Coordination Office (SECO), simulation consultation to Microsoft and the United Nations and lead systems engineering roles building various simulators and distributed simulation network environments internationally.

John has held various executive management positions, including Vice President, Engineering for a NASDAQ firm and CEO of a start-up that became a Top 40 defense and public safety company in Canada within five years.

John currently resides near Ottawa, Canada and works for Lockheed Martin Global Training and Logistics responsible for commercialization of the Lockheed Martin Prepar3D® simulation product.

For book errata, downloads and additional information visit http://www.theprimalsoup.com.

For Colette and Jack

Table of Contents

Table of Figures

1   Distributed Simulation Introduction and Overview

What is Distributed Simulation?

Distributed Simulation is the term for connecting people, equipment, and simulators together in a (common) synthetic environment. The simulation is dispersed on multiple computer systems that are connected together. Distributed simulation can be real-time or not real-time. It can be visual or not visual. There are many different ways of constructing a distributed simulation.

In this book, we will restrict discussion of Distributed Simulation to real-time, mainly visual, simulation across multiple host computers, systems and/ or actors.

What Does This Book Cover?

This book can be used as a reference, a planning and implementation guide, or just a primer for those considering options for solving problems using distributed simulation. I have included templates for some documents that I have adapted and evolved over time for use as planning and implementation tools for practitioners as well. Some of the lessons that are conveyed are hard-won or just seemed like common sense at the time. They may not work in some circumstances as each distributed simulation event will be different to any other distributed simulation event. Some of the frustration comes from this fact. You cannot necessarily "template" a solution onto a problem and certainly don't go through each step of a process religiously just because the step appears on a list. If it is not required, or seems superfluous, skip it, move on and do the stuff that needs to be done.

I offer tips and guidance throughout the chapters in the book and highlight areas that in the past have consumed most of the planning and implementation efforts. Some are critical and cannot be overlooked and have created issues for a lot of projects because they have been forgotten. If I mention terrain as the key to many distributed simulation exercises and you are nodding sagely as you read this, you most probably are still feeling the phantom wound of that injury!

Why Use Distributed Simulation?

The sum of the parts is greater than a single piece. Distributed simulation allows us to tap into the power of systems that may not be normally joined together. It allows us to have more people, organizations and systems involved in an event that could save money, resources and time. It can be an economical way to bring individuals and groups together in what could normally be a dangerous environment, such as training for war, or operating dangerous equipment in harsh environments. We use distributed simulation to train, answer questions and provide solutions to problems that may have only been answered through trial and error in the field, expensive research, or cost lives.

The power of distributed simulation comes from allowing completely different simulation systems that may have been built on different software platforms (also perhaps from different companies, organizations or countries) interact and communicate with one another; they can share information and effectively talk the same language. Although it has mainly grown up in military organizations, the standards, practices and processes are being adopted more and more in civilian applications and academic institutions around the world.

Uses of Distributed Simulation

There are many ways in which distributed simulation can be applied to solve problems, save money, enhance training and situational awareness and so on. Here are some basic examples:

- Collective and individual training;
  - o Networking of platform simulators such as armored vehicle simulators and flight simulators for training;
  - o Network of serious games applications for soldier and first responder training; and
  - o Connecting geographically distant organizations together for collective training.
- Simulation Based Acquisition (SBA);
- Design of processes, systems and equipment; and
- Doctrine development.

Planning and Execution of a Distributed Simulation

How do you get from concept to successful distributed simulation exercise? This book offers one approach to implement a distributed simulation exercise based on the DSEEP (Distributed Simulation Engineering and Execution Process), FEDEP (Federation Development and Execution Process) and SEDEP (Synthetic Environment Development and Exploitation Process) processes (these are covered in greater detail in Chapter 8), that is tailored for the specific outcomes that are desired. There will most likely be no surprises here for the seasoned practitioner, or project manager, but again, I believe that even the more experienced simulation engineers and managers can use this book as a "cheat-sheet" guide. This is all based on common sense and successful implementation of past projects that have used this approach. The DSEEP, FEDEP and SEDEP offer great checklists of tasks and issues that need to be considered. The only difference is in the application of these processes to solve the specific problem at hand and the use of the Distributed Simulation Agreements Document or "DSAD" to document and share the various technical and implementation details.

Standards

There are generally three major types of Standards that are used in distributed simulation activities. These fall into the following categories:

- Ratified international standards (IEEE, ISO, ANSI etc);
- Mandated national or organizational standards (Government, military); and
- Industry accepted standards (OpenFlight).

There can be confusion between ratified, mandated and industry standards and their implementation. OpenFlight is not a ratified standard, but has grown out of a model format that was originally published by a commercial entity so that other companies could produce models and software that worked with OpenFlight applications. It is now the most common model format used in simulation systems.

The most frustrating part of "standards" is the degree of compliance to a standard, whether it is an IEEE or industry accepted standard. What is on the label may not be a true reflection of what the system or software can do, or could be open to interpretation. Sometimes slick marketing will obscure the engineering reality of what a piece of software or hardware will actually do.

A case in point is the marketing double-speak terms describing a 1080p "compatible" television. This is not the same as a 1080p natively supported television. When you look at the fine print we find that it means that you can plug in a 1080p piece of hardware, like a video player or cable box to the television, thus making it compatible. The actual picture might be less than 1080p quality (such as 720p, or even standard television 480i: which is also called "standard definition" (SD)), but it is advertised as "1080p compatible". You think it is great until you plug it in at home and realize the picture is awful. The same problem is rife within the Modeling and Simulation industry. Many simulation systems that we deal with on a day to day basis only live up to a minimal definition of compatibility or compliance. Examples include claims of IEEE 1516 and 1278 compliance. We put the simulation software into our federation or distributed simulation and it doesn't work. When we investigate a little further we find that it might have one or more of the following issues:

- Only works with "RPR-FOM version 2.0 draft n" federations;
- Only handles one platform type (i.e. can only process aircraft and crashes if tanks appear);
- Sub-net masks are hardcoded;
- The software is only capable of handling version 4 of DIS, everything else we use is version 6;
- Crashes if more than four entities are detected;
- Only handles one type of dead-reckoning algorithm;
- Can only process flat earth terrain;
- Radio emitter PDU crashes the federation;
- Only works in Time Stamp Order (TSO) federations; and
- Many other issues that would cause us to tear our hair out.

These are actual real-life examples of some of the problems associated with so-called "compliant" simulation systems. Some of these problems have also been discovered only after spending many tens of thousands of dollars.

Terminology

Like many industries, there are terms, acronyms and unique language specific to distributed simulation. General distributed simulation terms are covered in the next few pages.

Synthetic Environment

The United States Department of Defense (DoD) Directive 5000.59 (1998) is the glossary for Modeling and Simulation used in a lot of places and where we find the first definition of Synthetic Environment. Indeed the Wikipedia entry for the definition is basically the same. Its definition of Synthetic Environment is:

Internetted simulations that represent activities at a high level of realism from simulations of theaters of war to factories and manufacturing processes. These environments may be created within a single computer or a vast distributed network connected by local and wide area networks and augmented by super-realistic special effects and accurate behavioral models. They allow visualization of and immersion into the environment being simulated.

I find it a little confusing and to an extent I would disagree with some of what is in this definition. I contend that a synthetic environment does not need to represent activities at a high level of realism. It only <u>has to provide enough realism to suit its intended purpose</u>. The sky could be yellow and not affect the outcome. You could spend a million dollars turning the sky blue with realistic clouds and other ephemeral[1] models and so on, but if it doesn't affect the outcome, then it is money not well spent.

The definition does not encompass another aspect of synthetic environments that also leads to much confusion. A synthetic environment has the following high-level attributes:

- It is different for each participant;
- It is different for each instantiation; and
- It is fleeting and not permanent.

Each computer could have the same software loaded on it, with the same terrain and environmental conditions. Let's be clear, they are <u>not</u> in the same synthetic environment, they each have a <u>representation</u> of that synthetic environment loaded on their computer.

An example to illustrate this occurred in a military exercise with using Microsoft ESP®[2] with F-18 aircraft flying a mission together. One of the aircraft was having problems intercepting a low altitude target. The simulators were running the same software with the same terrain loaded. After some investigation, the difference was that extreme high winds had been accidentally set on one of the simulators and there were no winds on the other. If we truly were in the same synthetic environment, this type of situation would not occur.

Each has a unique perspective of that overall synthetic environment. The computers send interaction, position or entity updates between them and that is it. Every time we close down the exercise and restart, it is a brand new synthetic environment; it is not the same one. The previous one is gone forever.

---

[1] Sunsets and other phenomenon that are fleeting and transient.

[2] Now superseded by Lockheed Martin Prepar3D®.

Simulators, Simulations and Models

A simulator is a device that imitates some real thing, state of affairs or process.

Figure 1. Mechanical Horse Simulator used by the British Army during WW1.

Simulators are what we normally connect together within a Distributed Simulation environment to provide interactive entities. There are many different types of simulators from stand-alone proprietary systems (such as the horse simulator above!) to platform-based interactive simulators for aircraft, vehicles, humans, and so on. Simulators can be controlled by humans, computers or real equipment.

The act of simulating something generally entails representing certain key characteristics or behaviors of an abstract system. These characteristics or behavior representations are what we call models.

There are three categories of models:

- Physical;
- Mathematical; and
- Process

A **physical model** is a real mock-up or scale representation of something. It could be an architectural model of a new building, or perhaps a 1 to 1 scale mock-up of a new type of infantry weapon.

A **mathematical model** could be an algorithm, formula or language that is used to describe a system.

Process models are processes of the same nature that are classified together into a model. A process model is designed to anticipate what a process will look like.

A **simulation** is a method for implementing a model over time.

Live, Virtual and Constructive Simulation

A term often used in modeling and simulation is Live, Virtual and Constructive or "LVC" Simulation. A distributed simulation could have any one or all of these attributes.

Live Simulation is defined as live people using real-world equipment in a training role. This could be soldiers using real weapons with blank ammunition, lasers attached to the barrel and sensors on their combat fatigues (like laser tag systems, but much more expensive!).

Virtual Simulation is defined as live people using simulated equipment. Flight simulators are examples. These are mainly used to enhance motor skills of the users to gain proficiency in the use of equipment or systems.

Constructive Simulations is virtual (computer controlled) people using virtual equipment inside a computer program. These types of applications are generally used to provide large groups of entities that can be used to supplement virtual and/or live simulation players. Subsets of constructive simulations are Computer Generated Forces (CGF) and Semi-Automated Forces (SAF) applications. The terms are interchangeable. In military simulations they provide neutral, friendly and/or enemy forces that are programmed to interact with other simulation entities in accordance with their normal battle procedures or doctrine. Some of these are able to provide many thousands of entities in the distributed simulation.

Entity

Entities refer to those identifiable individual components within a simulation. An entity might be a platform (such as a ship, submarine, aircraft etc), a munition (missile, bullet, torpedo etc), a human being, or another component that interacts with the simulation. Entities are not normally items such as buildings or trees but *could* be if there is a requirement for that item to interact within the simulation by needing to be destroyed or used within the simulation in some way.

Entities could be human controlled, or computer controlled. If the entities are computer controlled there may be some form of Artificial Intelligence (AI) directing their movement or reaction to stimulus.

DIS and HLA

Distributed Interactive Simulation (DIS) and High Level Architecture (HLA) are the IEEE standards that describe the protocols and methods that allow simulators to talk to one another. There are various versions of each of these standards. The latest at the time of printing are;

- IEEE 1278.1a (2010) Distributed Interactive Simulation; and
- IEEE 1516 (2000) High Level Architecture.

These standards are further described in Chapters 6 and 7.

2 Distributed Simulation History and Trends

History

Simulation is probably as old as warfare and civilization itself. Using wooden swords in place of bronze to train recruits in the basics of combat is a type of live simulation that was common in many ancient civilizations. In fact, King Tutankhamen had a wooden training sword buried with him in his tomb. Small military figures found in other Egyptian tombs are thought to have been used by Pharaohs and their Generals in the planning of campaigns or "wargaming" as we would call it.

More recently, modern wargaming originated with the military need to study warfare and to recreate old battles for instructional purposes to their officers. The Prussian victory over the French in the 1870-1871 Franco-Prussian War, is sometimes partly credited to the training of Prussian officers with the game "Kriegspiel". This game was invented around 1811 and gained popularity with many officers in the Prussian army. These first war games were played with dice which represented what was termed "friction", or the intrusion of less than ideal circumstances during a real war (this included morale, weather, what we now term "the fog of war" and so on), though this was usually replaced by an umpire who used his own combat experience to determine the results. The roll of dice is essentially still a factor in modern distributed simulation environments. We call this "Monte-Carlo" simulation, where the outcome of an event is determined by a randomly generated number, rather than the effects of a specific decision.

An early engineering simulation employed by ship-builders was testing of sea-going ships by getting crew to run from side to side and front to back on the top deck in order to induce significant pitch and roll. This technique simulated the stability of the ship in high seas[3].

What we could term "modern" simulation is generally credited with military innovation and necessity to train soldiers, sailors and airmen with the use of new technologies. Particularly new aviation technologies to train pilots and crew in flying, air to air combat, bombing and navigation. During World War One, pilots were introduced to the controls of aircraft by taxiing on the ground with aircraft that had their wings removed and replaced by short stubs. They would then graduate to full flight and more if they survived the first landing!

Instructors soon realized that there was a real need for training devices that helped pilots get used to more advanced techniques before getting into the air. The first of these devices was called the Sanders Teacher. It was a mock-up of an aircraft cockpit mounted on a universal joint in an exposed position and facing into the wind.

Figure 2. Sanders Teacher (c.1910)

In 1929, Edwin Link created an electromechanical flight simulator that moved with the inputs of a pilot sitting in a windowless box. It was designed to teach pilots how to fly by instruments safely. This became known as the "Link Trainer" (also known as the "Blue Box") and many were manufactured between the early 1930's and the early 1950's. It is estimated that more than 500,000 allied pilots were trained on Link Simulators during World War Two.

---

[3] The use of this type of simulation prior to launch would probably have saved the Swedish warship, the Vasa from sinking in 1628! See http://en.wikipedia.org/wiki/Vasa_(ship)

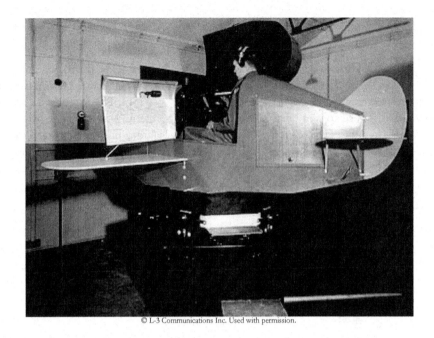

Figure 3. Link Trainer used for instrument flight training.

Computers began to be integrated with flight simulation devices as early as the 1950's and gradually improved performance and realism. Flight simulators provided by the large manufacturers were (and still are) very expensive and used proprietary hardware and software which is very difficult and expensive to upgrade. Military and civilian users spend many millions of dollars on single simulation systems that can only be used by one or two people at a time and require a team of technicians and operators to support.

As simulators became more realistic, military users began to see that simulators could be used for more than just initial flight and weapons training. They could be used for training groups of pilots flying together in tactical formations. This meant that the simulators needed to be connected together in order for the pilots to "see" each other. The simulator manufacturers provided basic proprietary networking mechanisms for this to occur and distributed simulation was born.

Of course, simulators from different manufacturers couldn't talk to one another. This was a deliberate policy so that their specific systems could be used and cheaper simulators could not talk to their systems for fear of them being replaced.

Indeed, when the SIMNET system (described further in this chapter) was first proposed by the US military to try to standardize interconnectivity protocols, it was opposed vehemently by the large simulator manufacturers and lobbyists were engaged to squash the initiative.

Timeline

The timeline below shows the introduction of various technologies, protocols and standards and their relative longevity within military and industry simulation environments. DIS continues to remain a popular protocol and a new version of the standard has been released in 2010. There are very few HLA 1.3 systems remaining, however they can still be found in some training environments. The box in the diagram below surrounds protocols that are currently in use within mainstream simulation environments. Service Oriented Architectures (SOA) is a potentially new direction for distributed simulation systems.

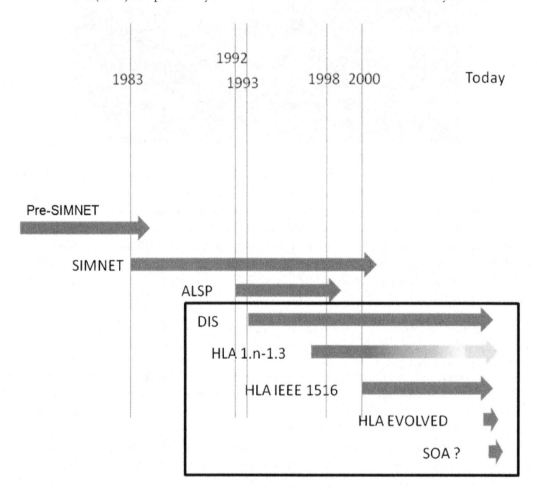

Figure 4. Distributed Simulation Timeline.

SIMNET

Simulator Network, or SIMNET was a United States Defense Advanced Research Project Agency (DARPA – now called just ARPA) initiative. SIMNET was a computer wide area network (WAN) that connected tanks, helicopters and airplanes in a virtual battlefield. Development began in 1983 and started to be fielded in 1987. It was used for training well into the 1990s until successor programs, became available.

Interactive simulation equipment at the time was very expensive, and the cost of replicating training facilities and equipment to multiple locations caused increasingly large training budget requirements. The ability to remotely connect participants rather than have them all travel to one place, hugely reduced the cost of training. The SIMNET long-haul network was run originally across multiple 56 Kbit/s dial-up lines with the addition of hardware compression to compress packets over the data links. The original network was designed to accommodate several hundred users at once.

SIMNET single handedly changed the simulation industry and has had profound effects on how the military trains and prepares for war. In 1990 ARPA handed over the SIMNET program to the Simulation, Training, Rehearsal and Instrumentation Command (STRICOM) and the program was integrated with the Distributed Interactive Simulation (DIS) program. (STRICOM is now called the Program Executive Office for Simulation Training and Instrumentation (PEO STRI)).

DIS

Standards for Distributed Interactive Simulation (DIS) were developed over a series of "DIS Workshops" held by the University of Central Florida's Institute for Simulation and Training (IST) in the early 1990's. The standard was based on the original SIMNET protocol and introduced the concept of "dead reckoning". This greatly reduced the number of entity position updates (and therefore network traffic) required to manage hundreds of entities. Detailed information on DIS is provided in Chapter 6 of this book.

The Simulation Interoperability Standards Organization (SISO) championed DIS as an IEEE standard and after a considerable amount of work by the DIS product development group within SISO, it became IEEE 1278 in 1993. DIS became a standard adopted by many international military organizations including NATO (STANAG 4482, Standardized Information Technology Protocols for Distributed Interactive Simulation (DIS)), which it adopted in 1995. It was intended that HLA be the replacement for the DIS protocol when it became an IEEE standard in 2000, however despite rumors to the contrary, DIS remains a strong and vigorous protocol and standard that is still used by many military and industry simulation users. A new version of DIS has been recently ratified as IEEE 1278.1 - 2010.

ALSP

Aggregate Level Simulation Protocol (ALSP) was developed as a result of a 1990 contract awarded by DARPA to the MITRE Corporation to look at applying SIMNET distributed simulation technologies to constructive simulation applications. A series of experiments was conducted and in 1991, SIMNET was extended to link the US Army's Corp Battle Simulation (CBS) and the US Air Force's Air Warfare Simulation (AWSIM) together. It was later extended in 1992 to include US Navy, US Marine Corps, electronic warfare, logistics and tactical intelligence simulation systems. The ALSP distributed simulation events were called "confederations".

ALSP created many key aspects of distributed simulation technologies that are now present in the HLA standard. This included:

- Object ownership. Each simulation controls its own resources, fires its own weapons and determines appropriate damage to its systems when fired upon;
- Message-based protocol. Used for distributing information from one simulation to all other simulations;
- Time management. Used so that the times for all simulations appear the same to users and so that events occur in the same sequence in all simulations;
- Data management. Allows all simulations to share information in a commonly understood way even though each has its own representation of data; and
- Architecture abstraction. The architecture permits simulations to continue to use their existing architectures while participating in an ALSP confederation.

In the mid 1990's DARPA transitioned the program to STRICOM and it became the genesis of the HLA protocol and standard.

HLA

High Level Architecture (HLA) was originally called DIS ++. It was produced as a merger of DIS and ALSP. In 1995, the US Department of Defense (DoD) produced a Modeling and Simulation (M&S) Master Plan to define the application of M&S within DoD. The first major objective identified in the plan was to establish a common architectural framework for interoperability and reuse. A High Level Architecture was listed in the plan as the foremost component of the framework. An initial definition of the HLA was produced in March of 1995 based upon industry and DoD user feedback and the first baseline was released in August 1996. As the sponsor of the HLA baseline, DoD produced its own version of the standard up to HLA version 1.3 (released in February 1998). Efforts to commercialize the standard and hand it over to industry culminated in the introduction of IEEE 1516 in 2000.

The standard sets out the rules and principles of HLA that are applied for distributed simulation interoperability. A new version of the IEEE 1516 standard has been ratified by

IEEE. While it was in draft through SISO, it was called "HLA Evolved". The standard is discussed in more detail in Chapter 7 of this book.

Although it was supposed to replace DIS for use within distributed simulation systems, adoption has been slow and DIS appears to have gained a new momentum lately. Perhaps this is due to the complexity of HLA implementation and the cost of HLA software and licenses from vendors.

SOA

The new buzz-word being thrown around M&S circles is Service Oriented Architecture (SOA). It is perhaps a future evolutionary step for simulation systems. SOA separates functions into distinct units or services. These services are accessible over a network so that they can be combined and re-used. SOA also incorporates People, Processes/Methodologies and Technology, rather than just throwing technology at an issue.

SOA does imply standards for interoperability; therefore HLA and DIS could be used within a SOA framework (and not necessarily exclusively or separately). The services that are provided to run a simulation system do not have to reside within a specific HLA federate.

The diagram below shows an example of a generic SOA model.

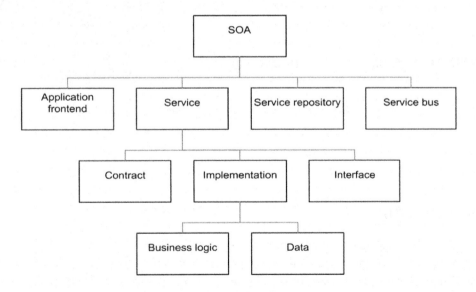

Figure 5. Conceptual model of a SOA implementation.

Applied to Distributed Simulation, services implemented remotely could be items such as streaming terrain servers, (entity) destruction server, weather services and so on. Applied to the extreme, HLA objects could all be considered SOA services which could be accessed over the network by any simulation requiring them. Although a full discussion of SOA is outside the scope of this book, SOA simulation systems are viable and flexible alternatives to purely HLA or DIS implementations. Practitioners of distributed simulation should look for opportunities to make services available (in the network) that can be re-used by simulation systems. It is a current trend in the wider information technology world that is being considered in the M&S world.

Network and Multi-Player Online Games

A discussion about distributed simulation history and trends cannot be complete without mentioning interactive entertainment games and the impact that each has had on the other. The history of computer and video games dates back to the late 1940's with a patent for a simple cathode ray tube interactive game. Later, oscilloscopes and televisions were used to demonstrate simple tennis and pong games. As computers became available to universities and research laboratories, they were used to program simple interactive games including text-based adventure games. Some key milestones are shown in the timeline below:

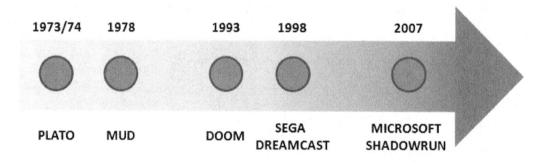

Figure 6. Key Network and Multiplayer Online Game Milestones

Empire (PLATO)

The first known example of interactive networked computer game was developed on the PLATO mainframe computer system in 1973. It was called Empire and was written by John Daleske. It was a strategic turn-based game for eight players. A player had a budget which controlled ships and industry and the ability to build more ships and maintain industry. Games prior to this were two player on the same computer or one player against a computer.

MUD

A Multi-User Dungeon, Domain or Dimension (MUD) was first introduced in 1978 by Roy Trubshaw. This genre of game was typically text based, where players read descriptions of rooms, objects, events, other characters and computer controlled characters (also known as non-player characters (NPCs)) in a virtual world. These MUDs were also played on mainframe systems and became popular on home computers as they became available. Some argue that modern online role playing games such as World of Warcraft and 3D social environments such as Second Life, trace their origins back to the original MUDs.

Doom

The first popular videogame title to release a Local Area Network (LAN) version was Doom from Id software in 1993. The first network version of the game allowed a total of four simultaneous gamers. A special mention is made of Doom as it is one of the first games to be used in a military training environment for the purposes of training soldiers. A modification of Doom called "Marine Doom" was released in 1996.

SEGA Dreamcast

1998 saw the release of the SEGA Dreamcast system in Japan, which was the first home game console to incorporate modem connectivity for online gaming.

Microsoft Shadowrun

The first multiplayer game that could be played between commercial systems of different platforms was Microsoft® Shadowrun© released in June 2007. This was a game interoperable between the XBox 360 console and PC. Arguably the PC has a Microsoft operating system on it; however give credit where it is due.

Game Network Traffic and Protocols

Game network traffic and distributed simulation traffic share common traits. Simulation and game systems are trying to send a lot of information across a network. Information is generally in the form of status, entity position and interaction updates. There have been various attempts to make game traffic more efficient and reduce network lag. Most network enabled games use either TCP (Transmission Control Protocol) or UDP (User Datagram Protocol) to send and receive information. Both of these protocols are very inefficient with lots of overhead to contend with. The game data that is sent is normally proprietary to the game company with little or no standards considered when describing an attribute. Some sobering statistics to consider:

Approximately 3-4% of all backbone internet traffic can be attributed to <u>only six</u> popular online games (figures from 2005). In a Korean study[4] of online game traffic the following information was discovered:

- In the popular Lineage II game of 6.29 billion client generated packets, only 1.44 billion (about 23%) contained actual game data. The rest was TCP overhead.
- With ShenZhou Online[5], TCP/IP packets accounted for 46% of all network bandwidth. TCP/IP headers accounted for 38% of all packets. Combined, TCP/IP protocol overhead consumed nearly 80% of all bandwidth from clients to servers.

There have been attempts to use DIS and HLA in the commercial game space in order to make game interactions more efficient and to promote a level of interoperability. Unfortunately these initiatives have in the most part failed to take hold.

Game Transport Protocol

A bright light in the darkness that is game (and simulator) traffic overload is an initiative to come up with an alternative to TCP and UDP. It is called Game Transport Protocol (GTP). It is being discussed in various online forums, however there are no standards defined yet. There are some academic papers written that describe how a GTP could work.

A contender for a viable GTP is the Stream Control Transport Protocol (SCTP). It combines some of the best properties of TCP and UDP and supports such characteristics as unordered delivery and up to 65,535 bi-directional streams. Benchmark results[6] for SCTP are shown in the table on the following page.

The results are encouraging and this could have extremely positive effects for the distributed simulation industry if it becomes adopted. Certainly an area that would merit further study by the industry in order to make network traffic more efficient.

---

[4] Kim, J., Choi, J., Chang, D., Kwin, T., Choi, Y., and Yuk, E., "Traffic Characteristics of a Massively Multi-player Online Role Playing Game". In Proceedings of 4th ACM SIGCOMM Workshop on Network and System Support for Games (Hawthorne, NY, October 10-11, 2005). Netgames 05.

[5] Chen, K., Huang, P., Huang, C., and Lei, C., "Game Traffic Analysis: An MMORPG Perspective". In Proceedings of the International Workshop on Network and Operating Systems Support For Digital Audio and Video (Stevenson, Washington, USA, June 13-14, 2005). NOSSDAV '05. ACM Press

[6] ISLAM, M. N. and Kara, A., "Throughput Analysis of SCTP over a Multi-homed Association". In Proceedings of the Sixth IEEE International Conference on Computer and Information Technology (Cit'06) – Volume 00 (September 20 – 22, 2006). CIT. IEEE Computer Society, Washington, DC, 110.

Message Size	1% loss	2% loss
30KB	SCTP 24x faster (than TCP)	SCTP 43x faster
300KB	SCTP 3x faster	SCTP 3x faster

Distributed Simulation Trends

This book has specifically shied away from discussing graphics and computer architecture advances. New improvements seem to come out with every monthly computer magazine editorial and there will be no surer way to make sections of the book obsolete before it is printed than to talk about current hardware. Suffice to say that each generation of CPU and GPU (Graphics Processing Unit) will improve distributed simulation in some way and make our synthetic environments faster, bigger and better looking. We must be wary however that we do not rely on bigger and faster hardware to solve inefficient programming, process or implementation methodologies.

The following general trends are observed:

Lower Cost Systems

Even before the global economic crisis of the early part of the 21st Century, many military and industry organizations have been looking at ways to reduce costs and stop building or buying single-use, proprietary simulators. Modeling and Simulation technologies in general offer a very cost effective way to increase training effectiveness, reduce costs in travel, hardware, munitions and so on, while increasing personnel safety. The costs for modeling and simulation technologies however have been slow to come down.

There are many factors affecting the cost, but as smaller companies become competitive in the defense and aerospace industry using PC-based technologies, the cost and quality of distributed simulation systems will come down even further. That is not to say that the total cost of ownership will come down to the same degree. There will still be to integration requirements, model and terrain development and so on, but the reliance on behemoth, proprietary, single vendor solutions will continue to be reduced significantly.

General cost trends are:

- DIS seems to be overtaking HLA in new simulation implementations because it is easier to use and cheaper to implement. DIS is far from dead and HLA has not replaced all legacy DIS systems. The general comments from the defense industry has been "if it ain't broke, don't fix it";
- Many vendors and users are shying away from expensive commercial HLA software licensing requirements and/or the complexity of setting it up, particularly

when they are having to implement many dozens of HLA federates with a cost of many thousands of dollars each on top of their existing simulation software application; and

- Open source software alternatives are becoming available for simulation users such as the Portico open source RTI, Delta3D, OpenEaagles and OpenDIS to reduce costs for some applications.

PC-Based Game Technology

The use of PC-based game technologies in distributed simulation will continue to increase and replace many existing PC-based image generators as lower cost alternatives. Game related interoperability protocols could also provide viable and compelling alternatives to DIS and HLA. Multiplayer game network and lobby management systems come already fully developed with features such as distributed physics modeling for destruction.

Game engines themselves are becoming more cost effective, sophisticated and realistic. I differentiate between the use of game technologies within simulation and using off-the-shelf games for "Serious Games". The distinction is subtle, but the implications are wider. Commercial game engines, such as CryEngine, Torque3D, UnReal Engine *et al*, are able to be licensed and used for non-game applications and provide a platform from which to develop simulation applications. Open source game engines, such as Ogre3D, IrrLicht and so on include source code that can be built upon and integrated with DIS and HLA protocol libraries. The Delta3D engine has HLA and DIS libraries already built in.

Commercial game engine developers haven't quite got the licensing model right yet for the production of Serious Games using their engines. The point of using such technologies is to produce high quality training environments at lower cost than the traditional providers of simulation software. A producer of Serious Games is not able to sell two million copies of their product world-wide to make $50 to $75 Million. It is more likely that the end user only wants one or two hundred installed copies for a particular use. Licensing an engine for $1 Million to these developers is unrealistic and shows that the engine providers are not quite getting the business model just yet. This should change as the industry matures. On the other hand, using an existing game and creating a modification (or mod) to the original game without changing the core game code is another mechanism that could be used if the game meets the basic requirements of the user group[7]. Marine Doom and Canadian Forces Direct Action (which is a mod for the Swat 4 game from developer Irrational Games) are examples.

Other technologies developed for and by the game industry that can be used in distributed simulation applications include:

---

[7] As long as the commercial license allows such use of course.

- Artificial Intelligence libraries;
- Terrain generation tools;
- Modeling tools; and
- Physics libraries.

3 Building Blocks

Introduction

In this chapter, we will explore the basic concepts and terminology of real time visual distributed simulation and look at what would normally constitute "standard" systems. The make-up and complexity of these will of course vary between implementations.   Some distributed simulation environments will be very visually focused with many out-the-window scenes, while others may be limited to plan-view map displays showing moving icons.

There are five fundamental building blocks that make up a distributed visual simulation system:

- Hosts;
- Image Generators;
- Network;
- Application; and
- Common Language.

There may also be gateways or interfaces that link distributed simulation systems to live or real platforms and systems. (This is shown on the diagram on the following page as a dotted line.)

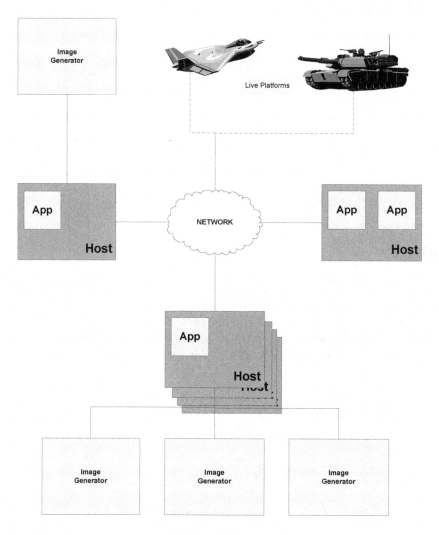

Figure 7. Building Blocks of a Distributed Visual Simulation.

Host

Hosts are computers or systems that communicate with the distributed simulation environment. An application (or multiple applications) resides on the host that communicates via the network to other hosts. To be a true distributed simulation, there must be more than one host. Hosts can include real equipment that is interfaced directly, or through a gateway into the simulation.

Image Generator

An image generator is an application that shows the representation of the synthetic environment. This is what you see as you are flying, driving, swimming or walking along when you are operating the simulator. This particular view is called the "Out the Window" (OTW) view.

The IG could be part of the simulator host, or on a separate computer system. In larger simulators, they are typically on separate computers that have powerful graphics processors on them so that the computer processing required is distributed. If this is the case, it is called the "IG Host". A simulator could have many image generators connected to it that provide different viewpoints, or a panoramic display.

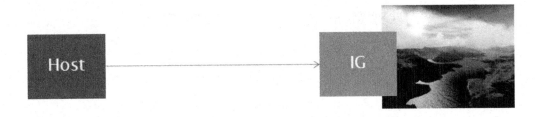

Figure 8. Image Generator is an application that creates an image for a simulation host.

A standard open source protocol has been developed for image generators called the Common Image Generator Interface (CIGI). This allows simulator hosts to interface with Image Generators from different manufacturers. It is scalable and can synchronize multiple Image Generators. More information can be discovered on the CIGI project website:

http://cigi.sourceforge.net/

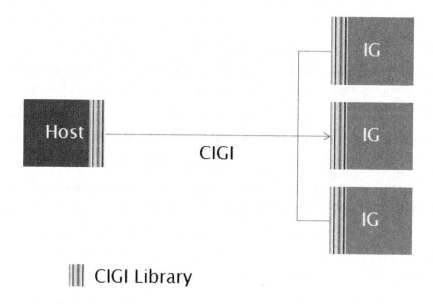

Figure 9. CIGI implementation for multiple out-the-window screens.

IG Master-Slave

Image Generators typically one system designated as the "Master" and all other IGs that are connected become "Slaved" from it. The master is responsible for ensuring that all of the slave systems are properly synchronized. The speed is generally dictated by the slowest slave IG in the network. IGs that are not synchronized can suffer from stuttering of the images and lag.

Some high-end graphics cards are able to use "genlock" (for generator lock) to achieve this synchronization at the hardware level. The video output of a specific video card, or an external source, is used as a reference signal to synchronize the signals. When they are synchronized they are said to be "genlocked".

A quick note on frame rates. The generally accepted minimum target frame rate (or frame frequency) for image generation systems is 60 frames per second (fps) or 60Hz. This will provide smooth rendering of the outside view with no visible lag or jittering. While greater than 60Hz is a good target, there are still some monitors and projection systems that are not capable of displaying more than a 60Hz refresh rate, so gains will not be noticed unless the hardware is changed.

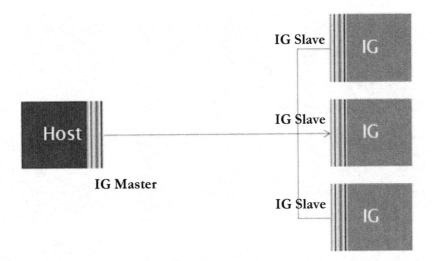

Figure 10. IG Master-Slave Arrangement

Network

In order for us to have a distributed simulation, we normally use a network in order to send and receive information between hosts. It could be a LAN, WAN, wireless connection, or other mechanism. (Just to be difficult, we could run a distributed simulation on one physical computer using multiple virtual operating systems, but let's ignore that scenario in this basic building blocks section.)

Application

The application resides on the hosts and provides the simulation logic for the distributed simulation to run. There can be more than one application residing on a host. The application could perform different functions depending on need or configuration. An example is configuring a single server to perform the function of HLA to DIS gateway, stealth viewer and logger. Each of these could be a separate computer program that each will access the distributed simulation environment separately.

The more familiar applications are the simulators themselves. A complex simulator can run on multiple computer systems with each computer controlling one aspect of the simulator such as a control panel or a motion platform.

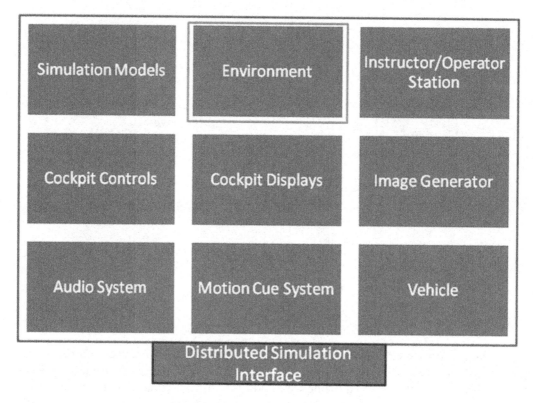

Figure 11. A look at a conceptual model of a flight simulator application.

Common language

In order for the distributed simulation to work, each application involved in the environment should be able to talk to each other. A common language should be understood by all participants. This common language can extend beyond using the HLA or DIS protocol standards. It can include voice, video, map symbols, terminologies and more. Protocol conversion applications may also reside within the environment to ensure interoperability between different applications. It is common to employ "Gateways" within a distributed simulation environment to provide protocol conversion.

Note that the terrain does <u>not</u> need to be common on all hosts. A submarine could interact with land based entities by firing a ballistic missile, but they will not necessarily need to use the same terrain. A fast jet fighter simulator will have different terrain needs than a dismounted infantry simulator.

Detail

From the five building blocks, we can start drilling down into more detail. When we put together a distributed simulation system there are some basic ingredients that are needed. This is not necessarily going to be the same for each distributed simulation system that is implemented, but it probably covers 95% of use cases. (The specific software, hardware, infrastructure and so on that we need to put it together are decided using the DSEEP, SEDEP or FEDEP process. This is covered later in Chapter 8.)

The following list adds more detail to what we need and introduces us to some of the standard terminology used in distributed simulation.

- Shared Purpose;
- Terrain;
- Own Ship/Player Entity;
- External Entity Representation;
- Object Representations; and
- Communications.

Shared Purpose and/or Understanding

It may sound a little too basic, but ensuring that participants have a shared purpose, or at least a shared understanding of what the goals and desired outcomes for the distributed simulation are, is a critical ingredient. Many simulation exercises that I have seen have been put together for the sake of putting something together rather than achieving a desired outcome or goal. Some participants have been confused as to what the end-state is for the activity is and left with perhaps true perceptions that it was a waste of time.

Terrain

Some form of terrain is normally required when putting together a distributed simulation. It is the "game space" where the simulation will take place. It could be the same terrain data for all simulators, a subset of it on some simulators, completely different, or not even required if the specific simulators do not need it to participate.

Figure 12. Terrain does not need to be the same for all simulators. In this case, the submarine may need to have terrain of the target, but it is unlikely that the ground-based entities will be able to target a submarine.

Own Ship

The virtual representation of the simulated vehicle or human that is being used by an operator is called their "own ship". Configuration files will normally allow a user to select a representative model of the equipment that is being operated, or a human model. The user may not need to see this model if a physical control panel or cockpit is available to replicate the equipment.

External Entity Representation

If the user is able to step out (or bail out) of the vehicle, then we will probably need to see the own ship vehicle as a 3D model. This is called the external entity representation. The exception to having an external entity representation is when the user is a Stealth Viewer and will be effectively invisible to all other entities in the synthetic environment.

Entity and Object Representations

Configuration files will normally (although not always) allow a platform specific DIS enumeration identifier (a series of numbers) to be transmitted along with the position of the entity. This enumeration ID is used by the receiving host system to attach the relevant 3D model (or 2D image if it is a mapping tool for example) from its library in the right spot so we can tell what it is.

If this enumeration is wrong, interesting and relatively undesirable effects can be generated, such as a tank model flying at 30,000 feet at Mach 2 rather than an F-16 fighter jet, or a C-130 transport aircraft racing along the ground firing at tanks!

Objects that we will need to interact with will also require some form of representation or model in the synthetic environment. These may or may not be DIS or HLA entities, but will still need a model. These could include AI controlled vehicles, humans and animals, trees, buildings, signs and so on. Note that some of these objects (such as buildings, trees and other flora) could already be compiled into the terrain model, so do not get confused between terrain objects and "other" objects.

It is not absolutely necessary to have the exact same model representation within each simulator. If the scenario does not demand a high level of fidelity, it may be sufficient to show a generic civilian four door vehicle model that represents all civilian vehicles rather than several different makes and models.

Communications

We will require some form of reliable network or communications backbone in order for the hosts to talk to one another. This could be a LAN or WAN over copper, fiber or wireless, or combinations of all. Security implications also need careful consideration and planning. Not only the content of the simulation, but the network security in place even if it is an unclassified exercise.

Some simulation systems require specific IP numbering and sub-net schemas to be implemented or they won't work. DIS and HLA have network routing requirements or limitations that will also need careful attention. This is a planning step that is sometimes overlooked.

Network Routing Schemes

These are four different types of routing schemes that might be used on a distributed simulation network:

- Broadcast;
- Multicast;
- Unicast; and
- Geocast.

Broadcast Routing

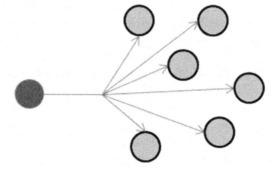

A message that is sent to all hosts on a network.

Multicast Routing

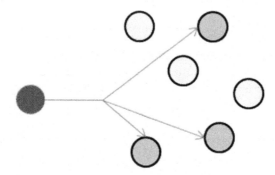

A message that is sent to a specific group of hosts

Unicast Routing

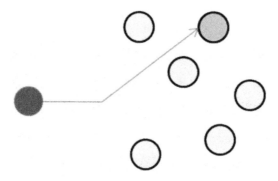

A message that is sent to a specific host.

Geocast Routing

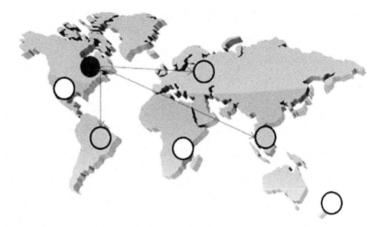

A message that is sent to hosts in a geographic location.

You will hear of the first two types a lot when we discuss distributed simulation. DIS is commonly referred to as a Broadcast protocol and is inefficient; however it can be configured to be multicast as well. HLA can be called multicast, but it is the "publish and subscribe" architecture that allows information to be sent to only those systems that want the information that makes it more efficient than DIS.

Latency

Latency is the length of time it takes for simulation systems to react from the time an operator, model or simulation creates an input until the system starts to respond to that input. Latency can be produced within a local simulation instantiation and on a network between simulations. It can also be known as "lag".

The latency in a local system can cause simulator discomfort if the visuals are lagging behind control or operator input. It is particularly amplified if the operator is using a head-mounted display (HMD).

4   Core Knowledge

Introduction

There are many terms and concepts that are specific to distributed simulation. Some are also common to the computer and console game industry because in both cases, the entertainment industry is working to solve the same problems that the modeling and simulation industry is. These include efficient use of resources across a distributed network, persistence of data, latency, "fair fight" issues, and so on.

The aim of this chapter is to provide introductory information that will assist in the understanding of common terms used in distributed simulation.

3D Model Format Terms and Characteristics

So you have found a fantastic freeware 3D model of a fighter aircraft on the Internet and you want to use it as soon as possible in your simulation. You export it to an OpenFlight format you think is ready to use in your extremely expensive simulator, you switch it on and it promptly dies a horrible death in front of the boss. You either do not see the model, your simulator chugs along at 4 frames a second, or it just doesn't start.

Implementation of 3D models in distributed simulation is unfortunately not as straight forward as it seems. There are a number of critical factors to take into consideration before using a model as an object or entity representation. The scenario described in the first paragraph is a common one played out all over the world (even if not publically acknowledged!).

The de-facto standard model format for many simulators is the OpenFlight format. The name is a little misleading as it isn't an open source format; it is the name of a commercial model format currently maintained by an M&S corporation.

The format is available and anyone can write an OpenFlight compatible piece of software. There are of course other model formats, (some which perform better) and not all simulators use OpenFlight, but most formats have the same characteristics and share common terms.

Model formats are a hierarchical structure like a tree. Different branches on the tree could be visible or turned on depending on what functionality is required at the time. The model used in a video game or simulation is not the same model that would be used by engineers or designers. These models are typically made up of many millions of polygons with sub-millimeter tolerances and are not meant for real-time simulation. (It would be nice to use that model as a basis for a simulator model, but in a lot of cases it is easier to build from scratch, optimized for use within the simulation.) See the figure below to decide which would be more suitable for real-time distributed simulation.

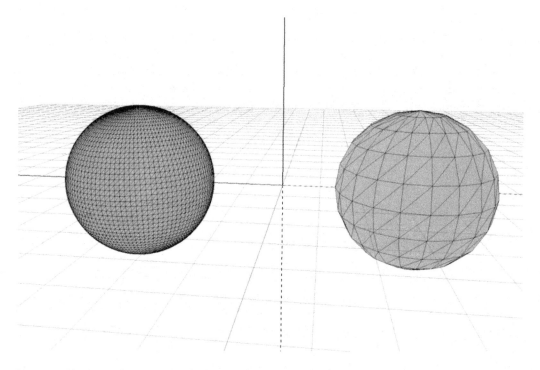

Figure 13. The lower resolution sphere will be efficient for real-time 3D simulation use.

The model used for simulation is most likely made up of several models of the same equipment at different states, articulations, levels of detail and so on. They can be nested several layers deep. It is up to the Image Generator to translate the structure of the file hierarchy into a viewable model.

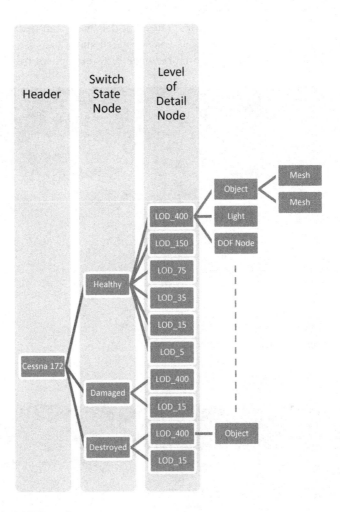

Figure 14. Typical Model Hierarchy.

As can be seen in the example above, the Cessna 172 model has three switch states: a healthy or undamaged model, a damaged model and a destroyed model. Each one of these states has a different level of detail (LOD) model that is shown depending upon the distance away from the viewer (explained in more detail on page 39). There can be many hundreds of components that make up each model below the LOD node shown. In this simplistic example the Cessna model is actually made up of ten different models, but could easily have 18 if we decided to use the same amount of LODs in the "Healthy" model per switch state!

Switch State

A Switch State is triggered when the object is required to change form in some way. It is typically used to swap out a healthy model for something that is damaged or destroyed in a battlefield when it gets hit by a munition. These model swaps can be hidden by an explosion and smoke when the munition strikes. Switch states can also be used to show helicopter rotors static, or rotating, switch between different sensor modes and so on.

Figure 15. Undamaged model switch state.

Figure 16. Damaged model switch state.

Figure 17. Destroyed model switch state.

A trick that is employed regularly to differentiate between healthy and damaged states is to simply use a different texture to indicate damage rather than change the model geometry. Artists use scorch mark on the textures and bullet hole "decals" and can be very effective when used skillfully.

Level of Detail (LOD)

Distributed simulation requires optimizations wherever possible to improve performance. One of the critical performance increases for an image generator can be achieved by scaling back the number of polygons needed to draw the model. Each polygon that needs to be drawn requires processing power. The less polygons, the better the performance of the computer.

There is absolutely no point in drawing antenna masts, wheel nuts and door handles on a vehicle if it is a thousand feet away because you won't see these details (in any case, there probably aren't enough pixels in the display to show these anyway).

The Level of Detail (LOD) is a method in which the number of polygons is reduced in a model the further away the model is from the viewer. The lowest level of detail is typically a few simple shapes that loosely resemble the original model. A typical model will have four or five LOD nodes per switch state.

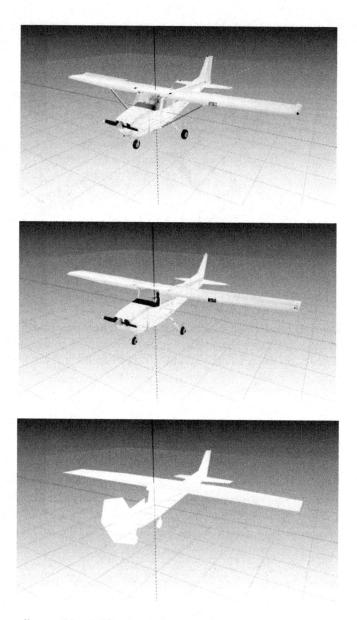

Figure 18. High, medium and low LOD.

Each LOD will have a "switch in" distance and a "switch out" distance that will determine when the LOD will be shown. These are set within the modeling tool being used. Most software will also use a method of gradually dissolving one LOD into another to ensure a smooth transition between LODs. (Also known as "Alpha Blending".) This prevents LOD "popping" where one LOD is suddenly swapped out for another. (Overlapping the switch in and switch out distances of the different LODs may mitigate LOD popping if the simulation software does not handle it gracefully.)

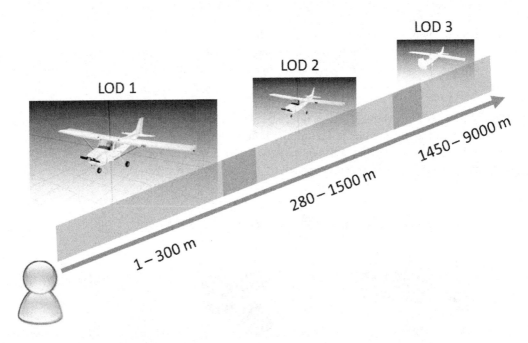

Figure 19. Arbitrary LOD switch in/out distances showing overlap.

Degree Of Freedom (DOF) for Models

In an OpenFlight model, a degree of freedom (DOF) is used to determine the articulation of an object part with a minimum and maximum limit of its movement. These movements are applied to the movement of the part in the X, Y and Z axis from its origin. This type of node in a model format is used to move things like hatches, turrets, landing gear and so on. A DIS and HLA simulated entity can send information over the network with the position of articulated parts so that participants can tell if things like tank main guns are pointed towards you, or away from you, which is important information to have! You will also hear the term DOF being applied to a simulator motion platform. This is described further in the book.

Sensors

A lot of modern simulation systems can simulate battlefield sensor systems such as infra-red[8] (IR) and night vision goggles (NVG). Some image generators can automatically do this, but the model will still require customization to ensure that realistic heat signatures are incorporated into it. Image generator documentation should describe the model requirements and there are modeling tools that allow users to generate realistic thermal characteristics from their model.

The shortcut way to do this if a user does not have access to IR or NVG model conversion tools has traditionally been to re-texture the model with a best guess at a heat signature or night vision image. (Classified and unclassified thermal signature reference data could also be used to generate an appropriate texture by the modeler or artist.)

Figure 20. Models with original texture, IR White Hot and IR Black Hot textures.

---

[8] There are two main types of infra-red sensors that are used. The first is called Infra-Red "Black Hot", which means that warm and hot areas are black. The second is Infra-Red "White Hot" where warm and hot areas are white.

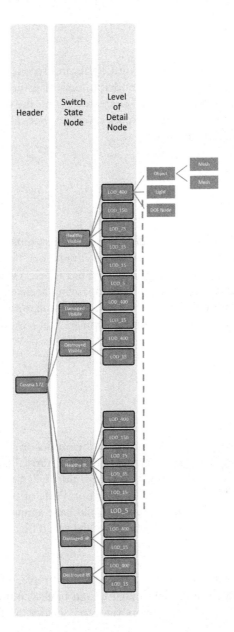

Figure 21. Typical Model Hierarchy with Sensor Switch States.

Now that an infrared sensor state has been added into the model hierarchy we have now doubled the number of models required to 20. If we decided to use the same number of LOD's in our "Healthy" model, we could have 36 distinct models that make up our one Cessna!

Attach Points

Special effects such as smoke, fire, sound, lights and so on, are generally created by the image generator that is showing the model. In order for the image generator to know where to put these effects, an "attach point" is created within the model. These points will normally have a specific naming convention so that they do not conflict with other geometry contained in the model.

Model Licensing

A mention of licensing must be made. M&S specialists must be aware of the license conditions of models within their distributed simulation. These license conditions vary from developer to developer and sometimes model to model. Assumptions cannot be made on the use of models; you must read any accompanying license agreement. Do not assume that you can just take a model from one computer or simulator and use it on another even if you have already paid for it. Some developers stipulate that a model can only be used on a seat by seat basis.

Fidelity

This term is used to describe to what degree the model or simulation reproduces the state or behavior of its real-world counterpart. Fidelity is normally described as high, medium or low. If the model or simulation is labeled "high fidelity", it is a very close representation of the real-world item. If it is "low fidelity" it is not. Parts of the same simulation system could have different fidelities. A flight simulator could have actual aircraft flight controls so these could be called high fidelity, but the flight model could be only an approximation of the aircraft being flown.

Fidelity can be very subjective term. In the above example, a human factors group studying flight controls would consider the simulator high fidelity, but an aerodynamics engineer would consider it low fidelity. It is important to consider the fidelity of each system component.

Objective, measurable fidelity requirements are specified for certified flight simulators and training devices. There are various national government aviation agencies around the world that have qualification programmes for flight simulators. Many of these follow the United States Federal Aviation Authority (FAA) or European Joint Aviation Authorities (JAA) standards.

Note that there are no specific government qualification standards for other types of simulated platforms such as heavy equipment, cars, trucks, and so on.

Flight Simulator Qualification

Flight simulators are grouped into different types of training device. These are:

- **Cockpit Procedures Trainer (CPT).** These are used to practice basic cockpit procedures such as start-up checklists, emergency procedures and so on and for basic cockpit familiarization. CPTs are normally not regulated;
- **Aviation Training Device (ATD).** These devices are used for the basic training of generic flight concepts and procedures. They would employ a generic flight model and use common flight instruments;
- **Basic Instrument Training Device (BITD).** A basic device used for generic instrument flight procedures;
- **Flight and Navigation Procedures Trainer (FNPT).** These are used for generic flight training. Although generic, they would normally require a good flight model with many systems and environmental effects also implemented;
- **Flight Training Device (FTD).** These simulators could be generic, or aircraft specific. They will have comprehensive flight, systems and environmental models. High level FTDs require visual systems to be implemented; and
- **Full Flight Simulator (FFS).** These are used for specific aircraft flight training. All relevant systems must be fully simulated and a high fidelity flight model is required. All FFS require visual systems.

Note that there are slight differences between the FAA and JAA terminologies for the above descriptions. FAA simulator qualification[9] is described in 14 CFR Part 60 (Title 14 of the Code of Federal Regulations). JAA simulator qualification is described in (Joint Aviation Requirements) JAR-FSTD A (Airplane) and JAR-FSTD H (Helicopter).

Qualification levels that are currently used by FAA and JAA are listed below very broadly. The umbrella term for all of these simulators is Flight Simulation Training Device (FSTD).

FAA

FTD

- **Level 4.** Helicopter only. Similar to a Cockpit Procedures Trainer. It does not require an aerodynamic model, but does require accurate systems modeling;

---

[9] "Certification" is no longer used when describing approval for these flight simulation devices, it has been replaced by the term Qualification.

- **Level 5.** Aerodynamic programming and systems modeling is required. It could represent a family of aircraft and does not need to be a specific model;
- **Level 6**[10]**.** Aircraft model specific aerodynamic programming, control feel and physical cockpit are required; and
- **Level 7.** Helicopter only. Model specific. All applicable aerodynamics, flight controls and systems must be modeled. A vibration system must be supplied and this is the first level to require a visual system.

<u>FFS</u>

- **Level A.** Airplane only. The lowest level of full flight simulator. This is the first level for which a motion system is required. A full scale replica cockpit is used;
- **Level B.** Requires a higher fidelity aerodynamic model than Level A. This is the lowest level of helicopter flight simulator;
- **Level C.** Requires increase response (a lower transport delay or latency) over lower levels. Visual systems requirements are more stringent; and
- **Level D.** The highest level of FSTD qualification available. The first level for which objective evaluation of sounds is required. A number of special motion and visual effects are also required.

JAA

<u>FNPT</u>

- **Level I.** Aerodynamics model of a class of aircraft is acceptable. Systems modeling only for the class of aircraft being simulated or required for training;
- **Level II.** Aerodynamic programming and systems modeling is required. Includes ground handling characteristics;
- **Level III.** Helicopter Only. Aerodynamic programming and systems modeling is required. Means for testing hardware and software. Minimum visual field of view of 150 degrees horizontal and 60 degrees vertical; and
- **MCC.** This allows for level II and III FNPT to be used for multi-crew cooperation training.

---

[10] Note that there is a significant jump in fidelity (and therefore cost) requirements to go from a Level 5 to a Level 6 FTD.

FTD

- **Level 1.** Aerodynamic and environment modeling sufficient to permit accurate systems operation. Electronically displayed instruments with an overlay are acceptable;
- **Level 2.** Aerodynamic programming and systems modeling is required, but need not be based on flight test data. Flight deck sounds required; and
- **Level 3.** Helicopter only. Atmospheric models required. Self testing hardware and software required to ensure compliance. Minimum visual field of view of 150 degrees horizontal and 60 degrees vertical.

FFS

- **Level A.** The lowest level of full flight simulator. This is the first level for which a motion system is required. A fully enclosed flight deck is used. A generic aerodynamics model could be used sufficient to meet training objectives;
- **Level B.** For an airplane, the motion system must have a minimum of 3 degrees of freedom. (pitch, roll and heave). Helicopters require a 6 degree of freedom platform at this level. A more advanced aerodynamics model is required;
- **Level C.** Self testing hardware and software required to ensure compliance. More advanced motion, visual and sound requirements; and
- **Level D.** The highest level of FSTD qualification available. Helicopters require simulated vibrations in the seat, flight controls and panels.

Qualification Procedure

If you want to get your flight simulation training device qualified for use for training, it will need to be evaluated by the national aviation authority in the country that the device will be used in. In Canada for example, the simulator would be evaluated by qualified Transport Canada staff. The steps for qualification are outlined in Transport Canada document TP9865[11].

Qualification is important if you want the device to count as loggable hours for a pilot. An unqualified device cannot be used to log flight hours.

---

[11] http://www.tc.gc.ca/civilaviation/publications/tp9685/menu.htm

The device will be evaluated against a set of criteria contained within the appropriate regulation governing FSTDs. Tests are conducted on the device and can be subjective and objective. The FAA publishes a Qualification Test Guide (QTG) that is used to record the results of the tests along with other information on the FSTD.

The baseline performance of the testing is called the Master QTG. Subsequent tests, which are conducted on a regular basis, record results against the Master QTG. If the subsequent tests are significantly different than the Master QTG results, the qualification may be lost for the device. Care must be taken that a simulator that has been qualified in one country can be used in another for training purposes. Unless bi-lateral agreements exist between the aviation authorities in the different countries, simulator qualifications may not be transferrable. Indeed flight crews trained in another country may not have hours credited in their home country if the simulator is not qualified in both.

Each simulator is individually tested and must pass the specific qualification criteria in order for it to be officially qualified for use.

Degree of Freedom for Motion Platforms

There are various types and configurations of motion platform commercially available. The two types typically used are hydraulic and electrical. Sizes can also range from single seat motion systems through to those that can carry many tonnes of load. A full description of how these systems work is outside of the scope of this book, however the term "degrees of freedom" is one that will be used regularly in the modeling and simulation industry. It is the same concept as a 3D model DOF; however it applies to the motion of the simulator rather than an individual part.

The degrees of freedom of a rigid body are described in the following table:

DOF	Description	Simulation[12] Term	Movement Type
1	Moving up and down	Heave	Translation
2	Moving left and right	Sway	
3	Moving forward and back	Surge	
4	Tilting forward and back	Pitch	Rotation
5	Turning left and right	Yaw	
6	Tilting side to side	Roll	

---

[12] These are nautical terms that have been repurposed for simulation motion platform use.

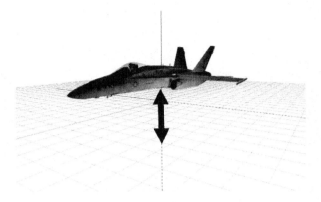

Figure 22. Heave.

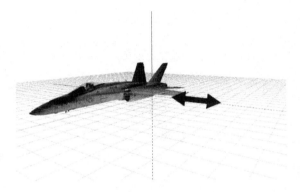

Figure 23. Sway.

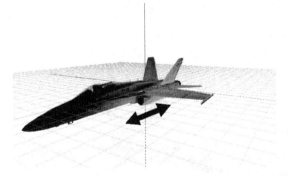

Figure 24. Surge.

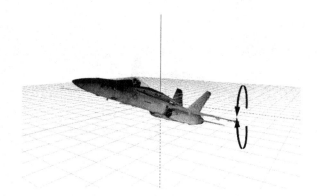

Figure 25. Pitch.

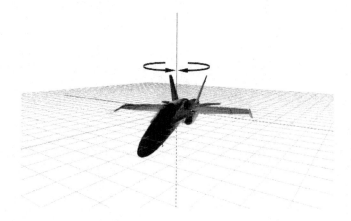

Figure 26. Yaw.

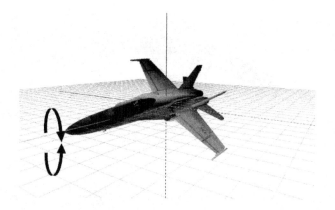

Figure 27. Roll.

Typical motion platform DOFs are 2, 3 and 6 DOF. The range of movement can be a few centimeters to many meters. (Some simulators can employ a small motor that gives a bump of less than an inch for the heave DOF. This can be an extremely effective way to replicate landing an aircraft, or a vehicle moving over rough terrain.) Combinations of Surge and Pitch can replicate g force acceleration and deceleration very well.

2 DOF

A 2 DOF motion platform normally tilts forward and back (pitch) and tilts left and right (roll). This is the most common and cost effective type of motion platform.

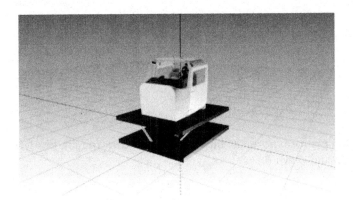

Figure 28. 2 DOF Motion Platform at the neutral/level position.

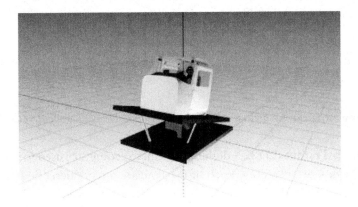

Figure 29. 2 DOF Pitch.

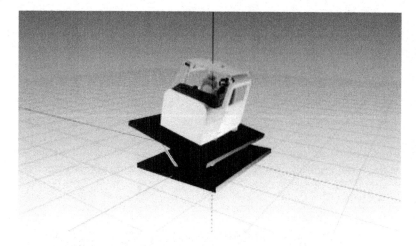

Figure 30. 2 DOF Roll.

3 DOF

A 3 DOF motion platform normally tilts forward and back (pitch), tilts left and right (roll) and will move up and down (heave).

6 DOF

A 6 DOF motion platform will have movement in all degrees of freedom. These are typically quite expensive and highly engineered systems.

Non-Flight Simulation Devices

Non-flight simulators can be grouped into the following broad categories:

- **Desktop Trainer (DT).** A desktop (or laptop) computer used to train a user for a specific task or operation. (Each of the simulation types described below can also be purposed as a desktop trainer. For example a Desktop Tactical Trainer (DTT), or a Desktop Maintenance Trainer (DMT)[13];

---

[13] The acronym combinations are many and will please many current and former military personnel!

- **Equipment Procedures Trainer (EPT).** These are used to practice basic procedures such as start-up and shut-down, emergency procedures and so on. They can also be used for basic familiarization;

- **Crew Trainer (CT).** This functions as a training device for equipment that requires more than one crew member. For example a tank crew trainer could have positions for crew commander, driver and gunner. It could be a series of desktop computers with each crew station networked together, or an EPT combined with a weapons trainer with more realistic controls;

- **Maintenance Trainer (MT).** These simulation systems are used to teach maintenance tasks and procedures for equipment. They can be virtual systems, or based on instrumented full scale equipment that simulate real operation;

- **Weapons Trainer (WT).** A device that replicates a specific weapon or weapon system. They can be used for familiarization, techniques, procedures, marksmanship and so on. They could be combined with other types of simulators; and

- **Tactical Trainer (TT).** Tactical trainers are used to train small team leaders (platform commander, patrol, troop commander etc) in the decision making process in operational combat situations.

The devices could be immersive or non-immersive depending upon the visual system used.

Dead Reckoning

Before diving into the specific distributed simulation protocols, a key concept to understand is "dead reckoning". When an entity moves in our synthetic environment it is moving in three-dimensional space. In order for an observer to know where that object is, the entity sends out updates on its position (in X, Y and Z) along with its velocity and orientation. These spatial updates are sent at regular intervals (up to many times a second) out on the network. Every application listening on the network uses those updates to plot that entity. Some of these applications will put a model of that object at those coordinates and that is how we see objects moving.

You can imagine that if we had many dozens or hundreds of entities all sending out spatial updates many times a second that we would bring the network to its knees very quickly. The other issue with this type of update is that the objects will tend to jump around between positions as the spatial information gets updated. Slow moving objects will tend to have smooth updates however fighter jets will teleport themselves all over the sky tens of meters at a time. It was quickly realized that a mechanism was needed to reduce network traffic and make objects move smoothly.

Dead Reckoning (DR) is a process of extrapolating an entities position, orientation and velocity based on the last known position, orientation and velocity.

The <u>Dead Reckoning Threshold</u> is maintained by the system that is sending the entity spatial information. If the entity moves outside of the calculated path threshold or tolerance, then it will send a position update to ensure that all systems are synchronized with the new actual position.

All systems will use the same dead reckoning algorithms to calculate the position of various types of vehicle. The receiving simulation system will move the entity around until it gets a position update and creates a relatively smooth movement for the entity.

The following diagram shows an exaggerated example of dead reckoning calculations on a helicopter. At the time of the first update, t_0, the helicopter position and velocity is calculated and broadcast and the extrapolated flight path is shown as the straight dotted line up to point t_1.

The DR Threshold has been set at plus or minus 1 meter from the helicopter's centre axis in all directions. My Sim is calculating the actual position versus the extrapolated position continuously. At position t_1 My Sim has determined that the DR Threshold has been crossed (i.e. is more than 1 meter from the actual position) and an update must be sent. My Sim sends an update that the true position is now t_1'.

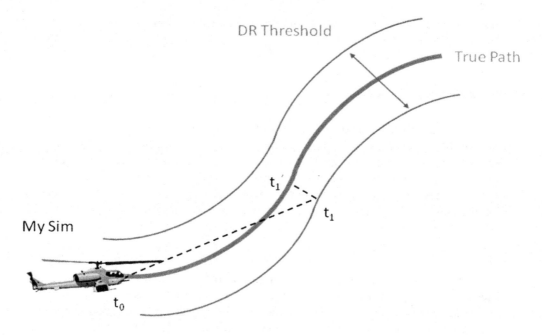

Figure 31. Dead Reckoning Example.

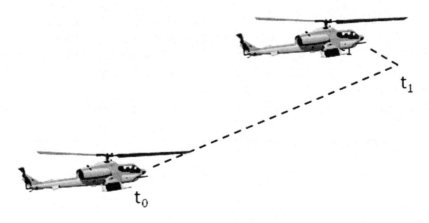

Figure 32. How other simulators see the My Sim helicopter.

As can be seen in the above (exaggerated) diagram, in our example there is still a jump of 1 meter as the aircraft is repositioned. A large DR Threshold will result in noticeable jumping of entities. There is a balance to be determined between DR Thresholds and network performance. An occasional jump of 1 meter may not be important to the specific exercise. DR Thresholds and updates are triggered also when an entity is making many quick maneuvers or continuous changes in velocity and position. A steady formation of dozens of fast jets will send less updates than a helicopter performing nape-of-earth (NOE) flying.

The following table shows the division of responsibilities between publishing and subscribing systems for DR.

Publisher	Subscriber

▸ Internally maintains:
  Actual value
  Predicted value
▸ Sends initial actual value
▸ At each iteration, calculates new actual value, and predicted value
▸ If actual – predicted > threshold, sends new update
	▸ Maintains predicted value only
	▸ Uses same algorithm as publisher
	▸ Predictions are cumulative
	▸ Each iteration, updates predicted value
	▸ If an update is received, predicted value is superseded by real value

Figure 33. Dead Reckoning responsibilities between Publisher and Subscriber.

Dead Reckoning algorithms (officially called Dead Reckoning Models (DRM)) are specified in the IEEE 1278.1 – 1995 DIS specification (Annex B to be exact) and are re-used in the IEEE 1516.1 HLA specification. The default DR Thresholds defined in the standard are:

- Position Threshold: 1 meter; and
- Orientation Threshold: 3 degree.

Example of a Dead Reckoning algorithm:

$$[R]_{w \to b} = [DR]\ [R_0]_{w \to b}$$

When planning a distributed simulation event, it is important to understand the DRM that is being used by participants. If you see entities moving in peculiar ways, a mismatch in DRM could be the cause.

Interactions

A quick note on the term "interactions". This is an explicit action taken by an object or an entity and/or directed toward other entities, objects and terrain. Examples of common interactions in a synthetic environment are:

- Moving;
- Shooting at something; and
- Explosions.

Time Concepts for Simulation

Understanding how time works in simulation is very important. Simulation time is not the same as wall clock time and we also need to have a mechanism to ensure that the simulation time is exactly the same for each system participating in the synthetic environment. Timing is critical within the distributed environment to ensure that data is received and acted upon before processing new events and interactions.

Figure 34. Simulation Time is not necessarily the same as the Wall Clock Time.

Here are some definitions:

- **Wall Clock Time**. This is the actual time in the real world;[14]
- **Logical Time.** This is the time represented by a simulation. Logical time is maintained by an individual simulator or federate. There are no predefined units of time, simulations will use whatever units are suitable for the system being modeled. Logical Time can also be faster or slower than wall clock time (also see Compressed and Expanded Time below);
- **Real Time.** Describes events simulated at the same speed that they would occur in real life. For example, if it takes five minutes for an engine to start and warm up, then the simulation model runs at the same rate and the engine will take five minutes to start and warm up in the simulator;
- **Wall Clock Synchronized.** If the Wall Clock Time is the same as the Logical Time, then the simulation is said to be "Wall Clock Synchronized". For example, it is 11 AM in actual time and the simulation is also at 11 AM;
- **Compressed Time.** The time runs faster in the simulation than the wall clock time; and
- **Expanded Time.** The time runs slower in the simulation than the wall clock time.

More on Logical Time

Simulation time is measured by ticks of the simulation clock, not by wall clock time. Each application will have its own timing engine and they must synchronize the simulation times to others on the network or federation. There are two types of simulations, continuous and discrete.

- **Continuous.** This type of simulation assumes a constantly advancing time and continuously changing system state; and
- **Discrete.** Discrete-event simulations are based on models that assume and unchanging system state until an event occurs. Once an event occurs, it produces and instantaneous change in the state of the system. In these types of simulation, time advances from event to event in chronological time order.

---

[14] It is good practice to actually have a clock on the wall when you are running a distributed simulation! It allows you to keep track of the real time as opposed to the time in the simulation. Particularly useful if the simulation event is taking place across multiple sites in different time zones. Have a separate clock for each time zone with a label underneath indicating the location.

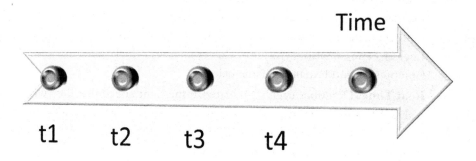

Figure 35. Continuous Time Simulation.

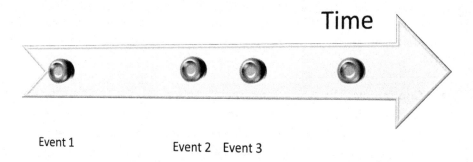

Figure 36. Discrete Event Simulation

At the end of each time step the applications within the distributed simulation will send and/or receive new values of attributes that are relevant to them. These updates are also called messages. HLA handles messages in a more complex way than DIS in order to control unnecessary message traffic. This is explained further in the chapter on HLA.

Time Server

Simulators will normally use the host clock to base their logical time on. This will be problematic if the computers in a network are not time synchronized and each have a different time. A solution to overcome this, if the simulation software does not take care of this, is to use a network time server[15].

Network time servers utilize the Network Time Protocol (NTP). We put an NTP host on a computer in the network and synchronize the other computers in the network to read the clock of that host. There are several software applications available on the Internet that can be used for this purpose, including open source and freeware applications.

---

[15] There are other ways to resolve network time issues, this is just one approach.

5 Terrain

Terrain Basics

Without question the biggest issue faced in the implementation of a distributed simulation environment will be terrain. It can be a critical asset which could take a distributed simulation from success to dismal failure in an instant. There are carcasses of many M&S projects littering the highway of failure due to terrain being overlooked or not enough attention being given to it. Here are some tombstone quotes that some readers may have heard just before the distributed simulation project spiraled into the desert sand at Mach 2.5 in a sputtering ball of flame[16]:

- "Let's just use the terrain from simulator x in simulator y";
- "We need 2000km by 2000km DTED Level 3 terrain at 30cm satellite imagery."
- "…and we need it next week";
- "I don't know what terrain I need….. oh, and the exercise is next week";
- "Season? We get a choice? Oh…umm…. summer? No wait… winter….why don't I get back to you"; and
- We will have a combination of fast jet simulators and dismounted infantry simulators so I will just use the same terrain on both so that you don't have more work to do. (By the way the exercise is day after tomorrow)."

There is some fundamental knowledge that will be required for terrain success. A high-level synopsis is:

---

[16] Most likely at about 2 frames a minute.

1. Get your terrain requirements gathered early!;
2. If you need to get terrain models built, get it done as soon as possible as there will likely be more than one iteration of the terrain as issues are identified and corrected;
3. Know the formats that you will need terrain in;
4. Know any limitations to the terrain models that you are using; and
5. Read this chapter 2-300 times.

Terrain Source Data

There are normally three data sources that we use to create a compiled terrain set for use within a distributed simulation. These are:

*   Digital Terrain Elevation Data (DTED)/ Digital Elevation Model (DEM);
*   Vector Map (VMAP); and
*   Imagery.

Using software, developers will combine these three types of data into terrain that can be used within a specific simulation environment. The end product is called "compiled" terrain. The compiled terrain can be in many formats. The most common is OpenFlight, which has an "flt" file extension. When developers compile the terrain, the map coordinate system appropriate for the terrain is also compiled with the data.

In a typical distributed simulation environment there may be multiple compiled terrain format requirements. Knowing what the various format requirements are early in the planning process is important. The image on the following page shows the various format conversions that were necessary in a Canadian Forces distributed simulation project that the author participated in during 2005.

The Canadian Forces Mapping and Charting Establishment (MCE) provided OpenFlight and TerraPage visual terrain databases for the project based on raw source data collated for the exercise. Additional format conversions were required by the end user for the various simulation systems that participated in the exercise. This was a relatively small exercise, however as can be seen there were six conversions necessary!

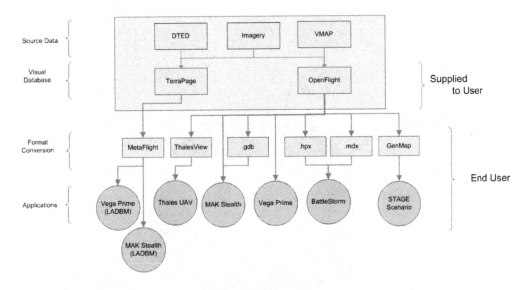

Figure 37. Typical terrain format and conversion requirements for a distributed simulation exercise.

DTED

DTED data gives us the height information for the terrain that we are using in our simulation. Without this data source our terrain would be flat. Digital Terrain Elevation Data was originally developed in the 1970s to support aircraft radar simulation and prediction. It is a standard of digital datasets which consists of a matrix of terrain elevation values. The DTED standard is maintained by the US National Geospatial Intelligence Agency (NGA) and is also described in the US *Military Specification Digital Terrain Elevation Data (DTED) MIL-PRF-89029B*[17]. The format is similar to USGS DEM files, however they are primarily used for military applications. (Just to be different, Canada has its own format based upon DTED called Canadian Digital Elevation Data (CDED)[18]. This is mainly used for civilian applications. Most military data is produced as standard DTED.)

DTED resolution is based on the distance between virtual posts on an Earth model. This is called the "post spacing". Different levels of DTED data describe the different resolutions. The closer the distance between posts, the higher the resolution.

---

[17] http://www.nga.mil/ast/fm/acq/89020B.pdf (contains the DTED format for level 0,1 and 2)

[18] http://www.geobase.ca/geobase/en/index.html

Figure 38. Concept of DTED virtual "post spacing" on the globe.

There are six DTED levels which are labeled 0 to 5[19]. Level 0 is the lowest resolution and 5 the highest:

- **DTED Level 0**: ~ 1km between posts (30 arc seconds);
- **DTED Level 1**: ~ 100 m between posts (3 arc seconds);
- **DTED Level 2**: ~ 30 m between posts (1 arc second);
- **DTED Level 3**: ~ 10 m between posts (0.3333 arc second);
- **DTED Level 4**: ~ 3 m between posts (0.1111 arc second); and
- **DTED Level 5**: ~ 1 m between posts (0.0370 arc second).

The issue to be aware of within distributed simulation is that the higher the DTED level, the more polygons are required to draw the terrain. The more polygons, the higher the computing resource requirements will be to draw it.

---

[19] At time of publication, levels 3-5 are proposed, but not yet in the Standard.

The following two images show the relative difference in resolution between DTED Level 1 and DTED Level 3 source data.

Figure 39. Sample of DTED Level 1.

Figure 40. Sample of DTED Level 3.

Processing of DTED Data

Raw DTED data should undergo pre-processing before it is turned into a DTED data set. Bodies of water are flattened so that they all have the same elevation. This makes it easier for software applications to identify lakes and rivers and color them appropriately. The rule is that all bodies of water with an axis greater than 1200 meters for Level 1 DTED, or greater than 600 meters for Level 2 DTED must be flattened.

Figure 41. Bodies of water should be flattened during pre-processing or unnatural side-effects will occur such as this hill effect on a central city canal.

The way in which the DTED data was gathered can also create issues with accuracy. Some satellite or aerial radar gathering techniques will not be able to see through trees and foliage[20]. The tops of trees will therefore be processed as the ground height creating errors that could be up to 50 meters out. Buildings and other structures could also be analyzed as ground and be several hundred meters out. (LIDAR can see through tree canopies). Pre-processing will normally account for such errors, however careful attention to how the data was gathered should be considered. Do not assume that the source data is correct.

---

[20] The Shuttle Radar Topography Mission (SRTM) data is an example of this. It provides elevation of the first reflected radar surface, which includes tree tops and buildings etc.

Figure 42. Example of trees being processed as terrain, causing a ridge in a city street.

Other factors that will affect quality are:

- Terrain roughness (how rough the terrain is between posts);
- Grid resolution or pixel size;
- Interpolation algorithm;
- Vertical resolution; and
- Terrain analysis algorithm.

USGS DEM/SDTS

The USGS Digital Elevation Model (DEM) (also known as a digital terrain model (DTM)) is a United States Geological Survey standard for storing a raster-based digital elevation model. It is an open standard. It has been superseded by the Spatial Data Transfer Standard[21] (SDTS), which is now monitored by the American National Standards Institute (ANSI). The two relevant file formats are:

- USGS DEM (legacy); and
- SDTS DEM.

---

[21] http://mcmcweb.er.usgs.gov/sdts/

This is not the same file format as DTED and care must be taken to ensure that the correct format for source data is obtained. Conversion tools do exist to convert USGS and SDTS DEM data to DTED.

USGS DEM data is classified into four different levels. (They do not relate to DTED levels.):

- **Level 1**: Created by autocorrelation or manual profiling from aerial photographs;
- **Level 2**: Created from Digital Line Graph (DLG) contours or equivalent, from any USGS map series up to 1:100,000 scale;
- **Level 3**: Created from DLG that have vertically integrated with all categories of hypsography, hydrography, ridge line, break line and all vertical and horizontal control network; and
- **Level 4**: Created from electronic (non-photogrammetric) imaging sensor systems, either active (e.g. radar or laser) or passive (received radiant energy).

VMAP

Vector Map (VMAP), also called Vector Smart Map or "feature data", is a vector-based collection of Geographic Information System (GIS) data about Earth at various levels of detail. Similar in naming convention to DTED, it has three levels:

- **VMAP0** (Level 0): This provides world-wide coverage of geospatial data and is equivalent to a map with a scale of 1:1,000,000. This is the lowest resolution. Coverage is divided into four geographic areas. VMAP0 data is in the public domain and can be downloaded from the NGA website[22];
- **VMAP1** (Level 1): This is a medium scale resolution range. The horizontal accuracy is between 125 - 500m and vertical accuracy is 0.5 – 2m. This level is divided into 234 geographical tiles. Some of these can be downloaded from the NGA website, the rest are not public domain, although some are available from commercial sources; and
- **VMAP2** (Level 2): This is a higher resolution data set equivalent to 1:50,000 scale maps.

---

[22] http://geoengine.nga.mil/geospatial/SW_TOOLS/NIMAMUSE/webinter/rast_roam.html

Data Layers

VMAP allows for the description and tagging of geographic features and attributes in different layers. These layers include:

1. Road networks;
2. Railroad networks;
3. Hydrologic drainage systems;
4. Utility networks (cross-country pipelines and communication lines);
5. Major airports;
6. Elevation contours;
7. Coastlines;
8. International boundaries;
9. Populated places;
10. Vegetation; and
11. Index of geographic names.

VMAP is used by many terrain development applications to automate a lot of the compilation requirements. It saves a tremendous amount of time if accurate VMAP data is available. Examples could include:

- Automatically smoothing terrain for roads and rivers based on the VMAP data and placing road and river textures in the right location;
- Automatically populating vegetation layers with foliage appropriate to the location; and
- Automatically generating buildings in populated place layers.

Shapefile format

ESRI Inc developed and maintains a vector data format called an ESRI Shapefile, or just "shapefile". A shapefile is actually a set of several files with various extensions such as .shp, .shx, and .dbf.

The format specification is published and there are free and payware applications that are able to consume and produce data in ESRI shapefile format. VMAP data is also available in shapefile format.

There has been a tendency to confuse VMAP with shapefile. "I would like the shapefile for Western Java" which is not so handy if you actually need VMAP data and your application isn't compatible with ESRI shapefiles.

Imagery

Imagery is used to provide a more realistic look to the terrain. Aerial and/or satellite imagery of the actual location is "draped" over the terrain as a top layer.

Resolution of the imagery is normally expressed in pixels per meter or centimeter. This is the smallest unit that maps to a single pixel within an image. For example, 30 m resolution means a single pixel in the image is equal to 30 m x 30 m of terrain.

The best civilian imagery available is 0.5 m[23] due to US Government restrictions. Typical simulation imagery is 2.4 m per pixel and down to 60 cm or more for some military applications.

Figure 43. Typical imagery resolutions used in simulation are 2.4m (left image) and 60cm (right image).

Imagery Issues

There are various issues to consider when using imagery. These include:

- How old the imagery is. Over time buildings are demolished or built, earthquakes and natural phenomenon change the terrain etc;
- Time of day the photo was taken. Ground shadows will affect the result;
- Season that the photo was taken;
    o Is there snow on the ground?;

---

[23] The GeoEye 1 satellite launched in September 2008 has 0.41 m imagery, but must down-sample to .5 m for non-classified use customers.

> o   Do the trees have leaves?; and
>
> o   Are the rivers dry or swollen?

- Were there clouds over the region when the imagery was taken?;

- Are there holes in coverage?;

- Is the coverage a consistent resolution throughout?;

- The higher the imagery resolution, the more computer resources are needed to process it; and

- Were adjacent terrain strip photos taken with the same camera? Do the colors match?

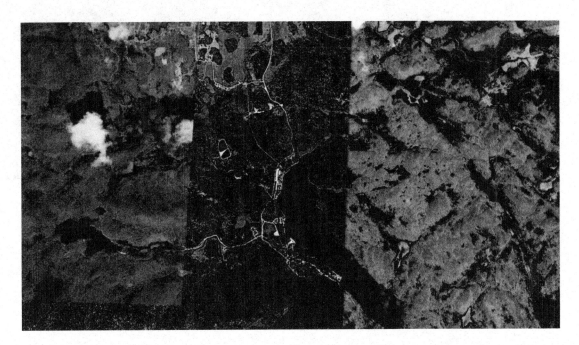

Figure 44. Satellite imagery taken at different times and seasons and combined into a single imagery overlay.

In Figure 44 above, you can see the effect of different satellite images being stitched together to form a larger image of a region. Various problems exist within this image. Not only are there clouds obscuring some of the terrain, the images were taken at different times of the day and different seasons. The black and white figure reproduced is not as dramatic as the color version which shows the terrain on the left and right as brown and the strip in the middle as green.

Another issue that crops up now and again is when combining different resolutions of imagery in order to optimize the simulation environment and increase performance. Higher resolutions are typically used for areas of interest, such as targets, supply routes and so on and lower resolution is used for all other areas. It creates a negative situation in what is called the "Postage Stamp" effect.

Figure 45. "Postage Stamp" effect in terrain. The higher resolution imagery is inserted within lower resolution imagery.

The obvious problem is that the user's eye is automatically directed to the area of higher resolution and if this is where the target area is, the user doesn't have to do much searching around to know where the bad guys are hiding.

Imagery Formats

The most common format for source image files, used in the building of terrain, is the GeoTIFF format. Geo reference information is embedded within a TIFF[24] file. This additional information includes data such as projection, coordinate system, ellipsoids and datum's. When a GeoTIFF image is imported into a compatible terrain software application, the image can be placed automatically in the correct geographical position and orientation without additional work.

---

[24] TIFF stands for Tagged Image File Format. This format is now owned by Adobe Inc.

Most terrain applications can use any common image formats such as jpeg, bmp, png and so on. If these source file types are used, they will be manually placed at the correct position and orientation (Geo-coded) on the DTED and VMAP underlying data. Some applications will allow the resulting image to be then exported as a GeoTIFF.

Other geo imagery raster[25] formats include:

- BIL: Band Interleaved by Line (used by satellite imagery systems);
- ADRG: ARC Digitized Raster Graphics (National Geospatial-Intelligence Agency – NGA);
- CARDG: Compressed ADRG (NGA);
- ECRG: Enhanced CADRDG (NGA);
- IMG: ERDAS IMAGINE image file format (ERDAS Inc);
- GeoJp2 (GeoJPEG2000): Open-source raster format; and
- MrSID: Multi-Resolution Seamless Image Database (LizardTech Inc).

Map Coordinate Systems

In order to find out the exact location a point on the surface of the Earth, there are two different coordinate systems that could be used. Lat-Long (Latitude and Longitude) and UTM (Universal Transverse Mercator). UTM is the system normally used in military simulation exercises.

Map Datum

A map datum is a mathematical model of the Earth which approximates the shape of the Earth. There are literally dozens of datum's used around the world. The most common used in North American military simulation exercises is the World Geodetic System (WGS) 84. The coordinate origin of WGS 84 is located at the Earth's center of mass. The meridian is located at the "IERS Reference Meridian", which is about 100 m to the East of the Greenwich Prime Meridian. WGS 84 is the underlying model used for UTM.

More on UTM

UTM is a grid-based method of locating points on the surface of the Earth. There are sixty zones specified and each one has its own transverse Mercator projection. Each zone is

---

[25] Raster graphics are resolution dependent. They do not scale up well without a loss in visual quality. Vector graphics by comparison are able to scale without apparent loss in quality. Vector graphics store images as mathematical formulae rather than an image.

further divided into regions denoted by a letter of the alphabet. The easting is the projected distance of the position eastward from the meridian in meters. The northing is the projected distance of the point north or south from the equator.

To locate a position using UTM coordinates, the zone is referenced first with the region letter, followed by the easting and northing coordinate pair. An example of a UTM coordinate is:

18T 0440253 5013770

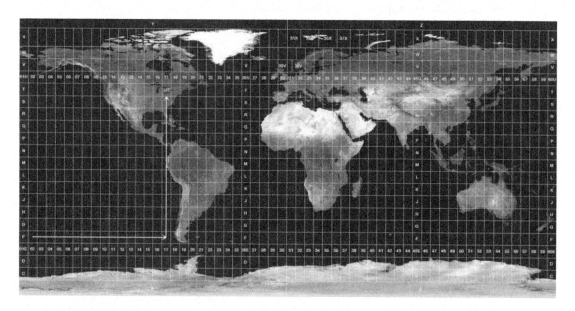

Figure 46. UTM grid.

Care must be taken with notation as it is possible to have the coordinate refer to two different points on a map. The northing distance could be above or below the equator. To ensure that this confusion does not occur, it is good practice to include the region letter rather than use "N" or "S" for North or South after the zone number. Some applications will also differentiate between North and South by using a "-" in front of the northing coordinate to indicate it is South of the equator.

Map Projection

A map projection is the term used to describe a method of representing the surface of a sphere on a plane or flat surface. All map projections will distort the Earth's surface in some way. A typical map projection is shown in Figure 46 above, which simply makes each line of latitude and longitude a parallel line. This type of projection distorts land masses closer to the north and south pole. A side effect is that Greenland appears to be about the same size as the continental United States, when in fact it is only about three times the size of Texas. Other types of map projections are shown here. Aviation navigation charts are normally in Lambert Conformal Conic Projection.

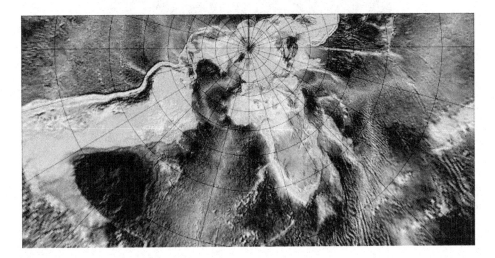

Figure 47. Lambert Conformal Conic Projection.

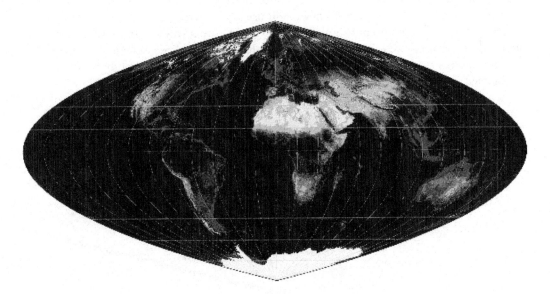

Figure 48. Parabolic Map Projection.

Figure 49. Orthographic Map Projection

Flat Earth Projection

Many legacy simulation systems, as well as some modern PC and console games do not use a standard map coordinate system. They might use a "flat earth" projection, which is simply an arbitrary x, y, z origin point (normally taken from a corner of the terrain) where all subsequent positions are calculated from. Some thought may have gone into representing real-world units as measurements (i.e. 1 virtual world unit = 1 meter), but that is not guaranteed.

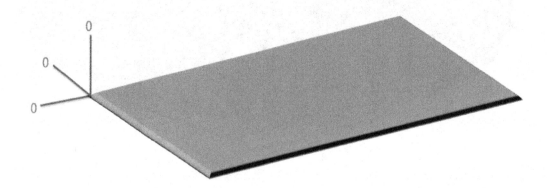

Figure 50. Flat Earth Projection.

Terrain Extents/Bounds

Compiled terrain will normally be received with Metadata describing it. The extents or boundaries of the terrain should be described. There are four datum points that should be given. These are:

- Upper Right (UR);
- Upper Left (UL);
- Lower Right (LR); and
- Lower Left (LL).

These are normally expressed as a UTM coordinate for each point.

Connecting Different Map/Coordinate Systems Together

There may be cases where simulation systems with different datum's and map coordinate systems will need to be connected together in a synthetic environment. If this is the case, conversions must be performed to ensure that similar points in each system will match as closely as possible. During the planning phase for the distributed simulation event, careful note should be taken of the map coordinate system and datum's used. Any differences will need to be resolved in order for the systems to be able to interact properly.

Terrain Correlation

This is the process of matching geographic points within different synthetic environments or simulators to ensure that the coordinates match. Best practice is to select three geographically prominent features such as a mountain top or stream/road intersection. A 3D entity model such as a tank or car is injected into the distributed synthetic environment from a reference application (such as a SAF) and placed at the known geographic point.

The entity will show up in the simulator from the reference and the origin offset is then adjusted in the simulator until the entity is in the correct location. (Typically this is a configuration file in text format that has a latitude and longitude setting for the terrain origin point. Adjust these settings by adding or subtracting from the lat and long will move the terrain underneath the injected entity until it lines up correctly in both systems.)

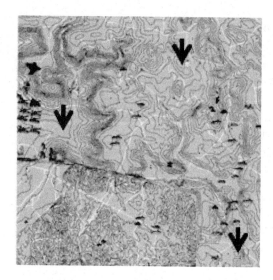

Figure 51. Insert an entity at three recognizable geographic locations to assist in terrain correlation.

Terrain correlation is critical for reducing "Fair Fight" issues that may present themselves during a distributed simulation exercise. If an entity is hiding behind a tree in their environment, but the terrain is not properly correlated, the tree might be 50 meters away in other simulators and the entity is now exposed.

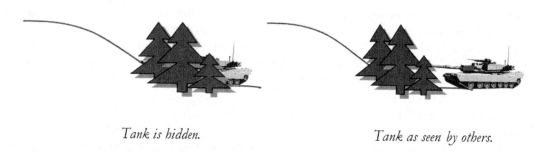

Tank is hidden.   *Tank as seen by others.*

Figure 52. Incorrect terrain correlation can lead to fair fight issues.

Other artifacts of incorrect terrain correlation include entities that appear to hover above the ground or drive through buildings and trees.

Figure 53. When terrain is not properly correlated we get..... Hover Tanks!

Ground Clamping

To assist with terrain correlation issues that result in different terrain rendering systems, "ground clamping" is used to force vehicles to be "clamped" to the ground regardless of their height above terrain. This solves the problem of hover tanks, but at the expense of adding processing overhead to the simulation for the additional calculations needed.

Ground clamping only solves height above terrain issues, not positional issues.

Figure 54. Ground clamping does not compensate for poor positional terrain correlation.

Terrain LOD

Just like the 3D objects that we use within a distributed simulation, terrain has different levels of detail as well. Terrain that is further away from the viewer is simplified and requires less polygons to draw.

A common problem with distributed simulation systems is that terrain and objects on the terrain might have a closer LOD switch-out state than an entity model. The result can be entities that can be seen at great distances when they think they are hidden from view. This may not be a terrain correlation issue. A building or trees that the entity is hiding behind might be in the correct position, but the building simply disappears when the LOD distance is reached leaving the entity exposed (and probably unhappy that they can be seen and targeted!). If the entity has a different LOD distance, they remain visible when their cover has disappeared.

The sequence of images below illustrates this effect as the terrain LOD changes. The viewer is moving away from the target and the terrain LOD is following the viewer. As the LOD's change, the target becomes exposed.

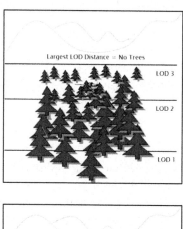

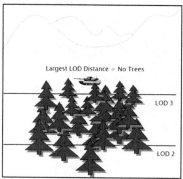

Figure 55. Terrain LOD's that are not synchronized with the entity model LOD can cause them to be exposed to view unintentionally.

Terrain Paging

Terrain takes up computer resources and memory in order for it to be drawn on the screen. Very large blocks of terrain soon overwhelm system resources in even the most powerful computer systems. Developers soon realized that if terrain couldn't be seen, there was no need to show it until you needed it. Terrain that is very far away can be drawn in low resolution and as the user gets closer to it, higher detailed terrain is loaded from the disk and drawn on screen. The concept of "paging" in terrain when you needed it was created. This means that massive terrain sets that can cover the entire planet can be used.

Autogen

Autogen is short for "Automatically Generated". It is used to generate buildings and foliage in some simulation systems. This allows for terrain settings to be customized for optimal performance for the graphics hardware being used in the computer system. The basic terrain model is unpopulated by objects and autogen settings allow the terrain to become more and more complex as the settings are maximized.

Autogen settings may be different for each system even if they are running the same software, therefore trees and objects may be in different places. This can be problematic in some scenarios, however it may not be important in others. Use autogen as long as it does not affect the training outcome.

In the pictures below, we can see the exact same terrain rendered in two different computers. The buildings are automatically generated and are not in the same places. This could present significant fair fight issues if it is a ground-based scenario.

Figure 56. Autogen can place buildings and trees in different places even if you are using the same software on different computers.

Buildings and Objects as Compiled Terrain

In order to improve performance, terrain developers may compile man-made objects and vegetation as if they were terrain. This includes buildings, telephone and power cables and so on. This simplifies the job of the image generator when it is displaying terrain, environmental and special effects and entities. The downside is that the objects and vegetation are not able to be affected by external entities or interactions because they are treated as terrain objects and are therefore static.

Modern physics- based image generators are beginning to allow developers to create more dynamic and destructible environments. Terrain destruction is different to building and vegetation destruction so compiling these objects with terrain may be a limitation in future systems. Be aware of these limitations when developing terrain requirements. Understand what needs to be affected by distributed simulation entities as this will affect how terrain is built and objects placed.

Dynamic Terrain

The ability to affect terrain and reshape it during a distributed simulation exercise is a very desirable feature. This can be in the form of cratering by explosions and the creation of trenches, berms and other earthworks at run-time. This is called "Dynamic Terrain". The affects of changes in terrain are replicated across the network to other simulators so that they have the same terrain. Changes in terrain can affect the outcome of events considerably, such as creating barriers to mobility, concealment from fire and so on.

Long considered to be a holy grail of distributed simulation, modern computer game technology now includes such dynamic environmental changes across multi-player games as par for the course.

Geospecific/Geotypical

Two terms for describing the type of terrain and imagery at a location are geospecific and geotypical;

- **Geospecific**: means a texture (i.e. an aerial photo) that represents what the ground actually looks like in a specific location. It could also include geometry of specific buildings, landmarks and vegetation that are found at the real location; and
- **Geotypical**: this means that the textures and objects used are typical of the kind of vegetation and terrain in the region, like grass, trees, desert or snow, but is not any specific place. Villages can be created that are typical of the types of dwellings in the region and placed on the terrain. (Geotypical doesn't necessarily mean lacking in detail.)

Each of these has a cost associated with it. Geospecific terrain is normally a lot more expensive to create as the developers and artists will be creating the terrain and geometry for a real place. This can involve extensive use of satellite and other imagery and sometimes field trips to take photographs of buildings and landmarks to use as textures for the geometry to make them as realistic as possible. The specific training objectives will drive the requirement for which to use. Mission rehearsal will most likely dictate that geospecific databases are used.

Compiled Terrain Formats

There is no specific standard for compiled terrain formats. This will vary between simulation systems. OpenFlight is a common terrain format used within the wider modeling and simulation industry, but not the only one. Other formats that may be used at times include:

- MDX/HPX from MetaVR;
- MetaFlight™ from Presagis;
- TerraPage™ from Presagis;
- ThalesView™ from Thales;
- OneSAF Terrain Format (OTF) from US DoD; and
- BGL from Lockheed Martin Prepar3D®.

Remember that these are <u>compiled</u> terrain formats. This means that they use source data (imagery, digital elevation data and vmap) to create the terrain and then they are published into a format that can then be consumed by an application after the raw data has been processed.

Terrain Database Creation

A generic terrain database creation process is shown in the following diagram. Another name for this process is the "Terrain Pipeline". Some applications are able to generate terrain from source data automatically.

In many cases the end result will still require manual intervention to correct errors, or place new features into the terrain. Terrain may also require changes in order to export it correctly to different formats. The diagram shown at Figure 37 on page 63, shows a typical terrain format requirement for a single distributed simulation exercise. It may require the acquisition of different terrain tools and software in order to convert to the formats required. This should also be considered during the planning process in consultation with the terrain experts providing the content.

Many modeling and simulation organizations have dedicated engineering staff, modelers and artists that create terrain for simulation. Some terrain is available for purchase pre-compiled, or can be sourced through central government and defense agencies responsible for distributed modeling and simulation. A criticism that I have is the lack of resource repositories (unclassified or classified) that many countries and organizations fail to create in order for resources to be found and re-used. There are many cases where the same terrain or models are created over and over again at great expense because of a lack of a repository. In one example, a company I ran received four different requests for the same model within a two week period. Two of the requests were for the same distributed simulation exercise and all four were from the same nation's Defence Force (and all four individuals making the request knew each other!). The problem would have been solved if a centralized resource repository existed. More on that further in this book.

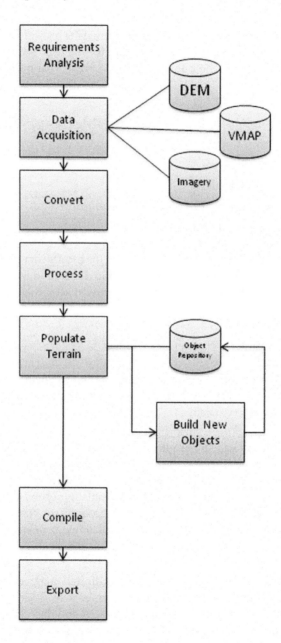

Figure 57. Typical Terrain Pipeline.

Emerging Trends

There are a couple of emerging trends in the way in which terrain is processed within distributed simulation. The first could be termed "Compile-on-the-fly" and the second is the use of a centralized terrain server.

"View From Source" Terrain

Newer technology cuts out the middle-man and allows terrain to be shown on an image generator straight from source data without it being compiled. Digital elevation data and imagery are used as-is and combined to provide a 3D view in the image generator. Disadvantages are that the raw data has not been pre-processed to account for anomalies in the data that might include holes in the terrain, misaligned imagery, flattening of water and so on.

Centralized Terrain Server

Rather than relying on copies of terrain stored on individual simulation systems, the use of a centralized terrain server that streams data is becoming more and more popular. Applications such as Google Earth™ and Microsoft Bing Maps 3D™ are examples of streaming web mapping services that show the potential of this technology.

Final Thoughts on Terrain

One of the major keys to success with distributed simulation is understanding terrain. This is a component that is often overlooked, or not given enough emphasis during the planning phase. You may start to appreciate why 99% of simulation exercises are conducted at 12:00 mid-day, in the summer, with no weather!

Plan for terrain early and perform a solid requirements analysis to ensure that the developers and artists have enough information to build or source terrain that will meet the objectives of the distributed simulation.

6 Distributed Interactive Simulation (DIS)

IEEE 1278 Standard

Distributed Interactive Simulation (DIS) is an IEEE standard that is described in the following documents:

- IEEE 1278.1a-2010 Application Protocols
- IEEE 1278.2-1995 Communication Services and Profiles
- IEEE 1278.3-1996 Exercise Management and Feedback,
- IEEE 1278.4-1997 Verification, Validation, and Accreditation

These documents can be downloaded for a fee from the IEEE website at www.ieee.org.

An additional document is provided by the Simulation Interoperability Standards Organization (SISO), which lists all of the enumerations used within DIS. It is called "Enumeration and Bit Encoded Values for use with Protocols for Distributed Interactive Simulation Applications", document reference SISO-REF-010-2006. It can be downloaded from www.sisostds.org. Enumerations are discussed further in this chapter.

What is DIS?

DIS is a peer-to-peer architecture that links real-time platform-level simulators together. A platform is a type of vehicle such as a tank, aircraft, ship and so on.

Basically it is a protocol that allows simulators to talk to one another. All data is broadcast on a network to all simulators. The receiving simulator can accept or reject the data depending upon their specific requirements.

DIS has a standard set of messages and rules which are formatted into Protocol Data Units (PDUs). These PDUs are used for sending and receiving information across the network.

The PDU type that will make up the majority of traffic in the DIS network is the Entity State PDU. This PDU represents all of the state information about an entity that the other simulators will need to know such as data about an entity's position and velocity.

A receiving simulator can use the position, velocity, acceleration, and rotational velocity data, to dead reckon, a vehicles' position before the arrival of the next PDU, thereby reducing network bandwidth (Also see Page 53). A simulator can also out the Entity State PDU as a "Heartbeat" to let all the other simulators know that it is still alive and part of the simulation. This PDU is typically sent at 5 second intervals, which is also one of the main disadvantages of DIS. It is sent even when the state of the entity isn't changing. This does nothing but clog up the valuable network bandwidth. The good thing is that this heartbeat time can be adjusted within most DIS simulator configuration files.

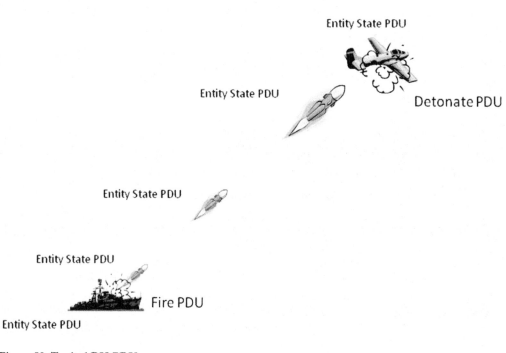

Figure 58. Typical DIS PDUs.

PDU Technical Information

A PDU is made up of a header and data. The header is used to identify:

- Protocol Version;
- PDU Type; and
- Protocol Family.

It is sent with each PDU so that receiving simulators know what to do with it.

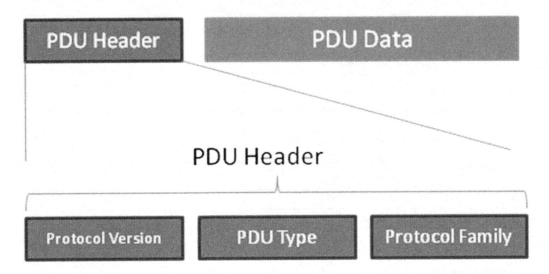

Figure 59. PDU Header.

Protocol Version

There are currently 7 versions of DIS and 8 field values used in the header.

Field Value	Protocol Version
0	Other
1	DIS PDU version 1.0 (May 92)
2	IEEE 1278-1993
3	DIS PDU version 2.0 - third draft (May 93)
4	DIS PDU version 2.0 - fourth draft (revised) March 16, 1994
5	IEEE 1278.1-1995
6	IEEE 1278.1a-1998
7	IEEE 1278.1a-2010

It is important to understand the versions of DIS that are being used in the distributed simulation. Some simulators will not function properly if they are unable to handle protocol versions that are different to their own. Symptoms will vary for interoperability problems caused by protocol mismatch. DIS PDUs will be seen on logging software being sent and received, however entities may not show up. Applications such as OneSAF and JCATS allow for options to broadcast and receive in specific DIS versions if required to support legacy simulation systems.

PDU Type

The most recent version of DIS (Version 7) has 72 PDUs which are arranged into 13 different protocol families.

Field Value	PDU Type
0	Other
1	Entity State
2	Fire
3	Detonation
4	Collision
5	Service Request
6	Resupply Offer
7	Resupply Received
…	…
72	Attribute

Protocol Family

The following table shows the field values included in the Protocol Family header (Version 7) information.

Field Value	Protocol Family
0	Other
1	Entity Information/Interaction
2	Warfare
3	Logistics
4	Simulation Management
5	Distributed Emission Regeneration
6	Radio Communications
7	Entity Management
8	Minefield
9	Synthetic Environment
10	Simulation Management with Reliability
11	Live Entity
12	Non-Real Time Protocol
13	Information Operations

Select protocol families are discussed in more detail below. The IEEE standard documentation should be consulted for full explanations.

Entity Information/Interaction

The data that follows this protocol family type includes the following information:

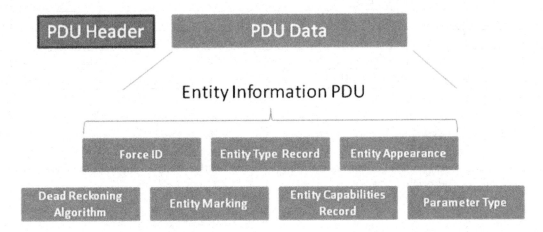

Figure 60. Entity Information PDU.

This information is normally held in a configuration file that can be edited within the simulator. This allows for reconfiguration of the data as required. Typical configuration files include the following information:

- Exercise ID;
- Force ID;
- Entity Marking;
- Country; and
- Entity enumerations (also can be mapped to specific models in the simulator).

Force ID

This field defines what side the entity is on. The Force ID selected for the entity is used in various ways by applications. For example, 2D stealth viewers will assign appropriately colored icons – red for enemy, blue for friendly etc to entities. Semi-Automated Forces (SAF) applications will also react to the entity appropriately in accordance with their programmed doctrine, by shooting at enemy entities that appear and so on.

If a SAF generated friendly unit starts blasting away at your entity for no apparent reason, the Force ID may be incorrect! (Check to see if your icon is red instead of blue when it appears in the SAF.)

Field Value	Force
0	Other
1	Friendly
2	Opposing
3	Neutral
...	...
30	Neutral 10

Entity Kind Record

The Entity Kind record contains further information on the entity to further identify its capabilities and origin.

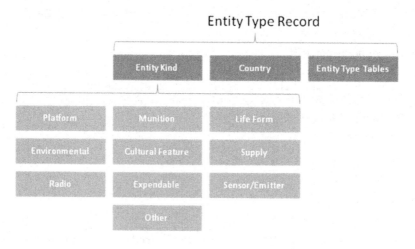

Figure 61. Entity Type Record.

The record identifies the fundamental characteristics of the entity. Is it a platform (tank, aircraft, ship etc), is it human, animal etc, is it an emitter? The table below is for illustration purposes. The full entity kind list can be seen in SISO-REF-010.

Field Value	Entity Kind
0	Other
1	Platform
2	Munition
3	Life Form
...	....
9	Sensor/Emitter

Entity Platform Record – Domain

This is a sub-set of the Platform entity kind shown in the previous table (field value 1). The entity domain type identifies to the simulator where the platform would normally operate. Some simulators will use this information to perform additional processing steps. For example, if it identifies a platform as a Land type, it might automatically ground clamp it, or if it is a Space type, it may ignore it and not show it (also see Filtering in this chapter).

Field Value	Domain Type
0	Other
1	Land
2	Air
3	Surface
4	Subsurface
5	Space

Entity Type Record – Country

The SISO document, SISO-REF-010, lists all of the country codes that can be used within a DIS (and HLA) distributed simulation exercise. The issue to be aware of is that country codes are associated with a platform's country of origin, NOT the country that is using the platform. For example, a T-62 may have been manufactured in the CIS (Commonwealth of Independent States - country code 222) and in use by Austria (country code 14), however the correct enumeration for the tank used by Austria is 222. This can get confusing for countries like India that use equipment from both the CIS and USA!

Standard practice is to use the country code for the user rather than the country of origin for the platform. Decide which country codes will be used prior to the exercise starting. This is normally done in the Federation Agreements Document (FAD).

Field Value	Country
0	Other
1	Afghanistan
2	Albania
3	Algeria
…	…
39	Canada
…	…
222	CIS (formerly USSR, so that is why it is a larger number)

...	...
225	United States
...	...

Simulation Management

The simulation management (SimMan) PDU's are used to control the simulation. The data that follows this field value includes;

- Start;
- Restart;
- Maintenance;
- Shutdown;
- Data Collection; and
- Data Distribution.

Enumerations

Enumerations are a series of numbers that describe the specific platform within a distributed simulation environment. They are normally placed in a file that can be edited for reconfiguration between distributed simulation exercises. DIS enumerations can be found in SISO-REF-010. There are some mandatory and optional numbers that make up the enumeration. The numbers will not be more than six sets of numbers long, but can be less if optional data is left off.

Using these numbers we can describe a US built M1A1 Abrams main battle tank. The specific enumeration would be:

$$1\ 1\ 225\ 1\ 1\ 2$$

Breaking it down further in a table, we can see how this string of numerals was constructed.

Kind	Domain	Country	Category	Sub Category	Specific
1 (Land)	1 (Land)	225 (USA)	1 (Tank)	1 (M1 Abrams)	2 (M1A1 Abrams)

There are times when enumerations will not have sub-categories or specific identifiers. In these cases, the numbers would be zero, or they may not be needed. This would give a set of four numbers instead of six. In some circumstances if there is only one type of entity from one country, it may not be necessary to show the Category field and it could be reduced to three sets of numbers. Also, if your exercise only had one type of tank from the USA, it would be acceptable to use 1 1 225 1, or 1 1 225 1 0 0.

Filtering

Enumerations can be used to filter out unwanted entities in simulators. This is done mainly for performance and sometimes for troubleshooting problems in the simulation environment. For example, a simulator may not be capable of showing ground entities, so all enumerations of (Entity) Kind 1 are discarded.

Another example where filtering may be used is if a particular entity model is causing the simulator to crash. It might be a bug in the image generator code that causes it to crash if a certain model effect is loaded with the model.

DIS No Longer Broadcast?

There are some research and experimentation activities being conducted to convert DIS broadcasts into multicast. Using sophisticated routing, these initial experiments appear to be showing promising results. With the cost and complexities involved in implementation of HLA federations, DIS has proven to be a tenacious protocol. The recent update of DIS in 2010 and with potentially a multicast capability coming, it could have a longer shelf-life than we thought!

7 High Level Architecture (HLA)

IEEE 1516 Standard

High Level Architecture (HLA) is an IEEE standard that is described in the following documents:

- IEEE 1516-2010 Standard for Modeling and Simulation High Level Architecture - Framework and Rules
- IEEE 1516.1-2010 Standard for Modeling and Simulation High Level Architecture - Federate Interface Specification
- IEEE 1516.2 2010 Standard for Modeling and Simulation High Level Architecture - Object Model Template (OMT) Specification
- IEEE 1516.3 2003 Standard for Modeling and Simulation High Level Architecture - Federation Development and Execution Process (FEDEP)
- IEEE 1516.4 2007 Recommended Practice for Verification, Validation and Accreditation an Overlay to the High Level Architecture Federation Development and Execution Process

The FEDEP standard described above in IEEE 1516.3 is currently undergoing revision. It is to be renamed the Distributed Simulation Engineering and Execution Process (DSEEP) and will be known as IEEE 1730. Publication is expected sometime in 2011.

What is HLA?

HLA is defined as a general purpose architecture for use in distributed simulation systems[26]. Interoperability between simulators is achieved by publication and subscription of an objects attributes between federates in a federation. Communications is managed between simulators through a "Run-Time Infrastructure" (RTI) application. HLA was designed to supersede DIS as the protocol of choice for distributed simulation.

There are three basic components in HLA. These are:

1. Interface Specification. This defines how the federate will interact with the RTI. The RTI itself consists of an Application Programming Interface (API) and a programming library. This specification also identifies "call-back" functions that each federate must provide. The API and library must be compliant with the IEEE standard. The interface specification is divided into the following service groups:
    a. Federation Management;
    b. Declaration Management;
    c. Object Management;
    d. Ownership Management;
    e. Time Management;
    f. Data Distribution Management; and
    g. Support Services.
2. Object Model Template (OMT). This specifies what the information is that is communicated between federates and how it is formatted and documented. There are two types of OMT:
    a. Federation Object Model (FOM); and
    b. Simulation Object Model (SOM).
3. Rules. There are 10 rules that the federation and federates must follow in order for it to be compliant with the standard;
    a. **Rule 1**: Federations shall have an HLA federation object model (FOM), documented in accordance with the object model template (OMT);
    b. **Rule 2**: In a federation, all representation of objects in the FOM shall be in the federates, not in the RTI;
    c. **Rule 3**: During a federation execution, all exchange of FOM data among federates shall occur via the RTI;
    d. **Rule 4**: During a federation execution, federates shall interact with the RTI in accordance with the HLA interface specification;

---

[26] http://en.wikipedia.org/wiki/High_level_architecture_(simulation)

e.   **Rule 5**: During a federation execution, an attribute of an instance of an object shall be owned by only one federate at any given time;

f.   **Rule 6**: Federates shall have an HLA simulation object model (SOM), documented in accordance with the HLA object model template;

g.   **Rule 7**: Federates shall be able to update and/or reflect any attributes of objects in their SOM and send and/or receive SOM object interactions externally, as specified in their SOM;

h.   **Rule 8**: Federates shall be able to transfer and/or accept ownership of an attribute dynamically during a federation execution, as specified in their SOM;

i.   **Rule 9**: Federates shall be able to vary the conditions under which they provide updates of attributes of objects, as specified in their SOM; and

j.   **Rule 10**: Federates shall be able to manage local time in a way that will allow them to coordinate data exchange with other members of a federation.

Federation

This is a term specific to High Level Architecture. It is defined as a system of interacting models and/or simulation, with supporting infrastructure, based on a common understanding of the objects portrayed in the system.

Basically this is the distributed simulation exercise that your simulators would join to play together in. You can have more than one federation on a network (as long as they have different names).

Federate

A federate is a member of a federation. Because it is an HLA term, you will sometimes hear people refer to a DIS compliant application described as a federate. This is not correct unless it has its own DIS-to-HLA gateway. Even then, the correct description is that the gateway is the federate joining the federation, not the DIS simulator.

Federates can be any type of HLA compliant application that is joining a federation, it is not just a simulator. Typical federate types in a federation include:

- Simulators/Simulations (Live, Virtual or Constructive);
- Loggers (records the simulation traffic for playback latter);
- Stealth Viewers; and
- Gateways.

Object

In HLA terms, an object is a collection of related data sent between federates.

Attribute

An attribute is a data field of an object. For example, a tank object may have an attribute called something like "position", or "damaged".

Interaction

This is an event sent between federates. For example, this could be a fire or detonate event.

Parameter

This is a data field of an interaction.

What Does It Look Like?

When a federate is publishing data, it is indicating to the federation that it is able to produce values for particular object attributes. When a federate is subscribing to data, it is indicating that it is wishing to consume particular object attributes.

The following simplified diagram shows four different federates that are able to publish or subscribe to object attributes through an RTI. The aircraft, for example is publishing its platform type (aircraft) and its position. The far right federate is able to subscribe to platforms of type aircraft and tank. (Of course federates are able to publish and subscribe simultaneously.)

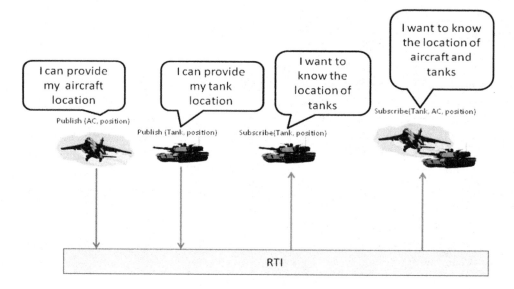

Figure 62. Simple HLA publish and subscribe.

The Lollipop Diagram

The lollipop diagram is used to visualize federates and systems that are connected to federations. It is a common way to draw federations and should be used when describing HLA distributed simulation systems.

Each circle represents a different federate on the federation. The rectangle at the bottom, or centre of a diagram should have the RTI version and developer in text inside it, or referenced using a legend key.

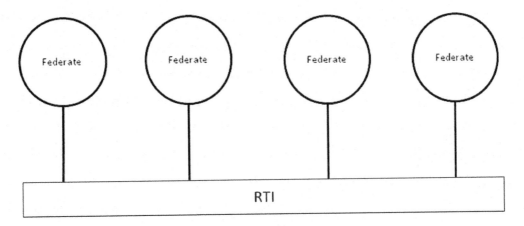

Figure 63. HLA "Lollipop" Diagram Federation Representation.

More on Object Models

The object model template consists of the following descriptions:

- Simulation Object Model (SOM);
- Federation Object Model (FOM); and
- Management Object Model (MOM).

Simulation Object Model

A Simulation Object Model (SOM) describes the shared object, attributes and interactions used in a single federate. There is only one SOM per federate. SOMs are used to ensure interoperability between federates and it shows what the federate is capable of. The SOM also determines how the federate will be managed, synchronized and what it will publish and subscribe to.

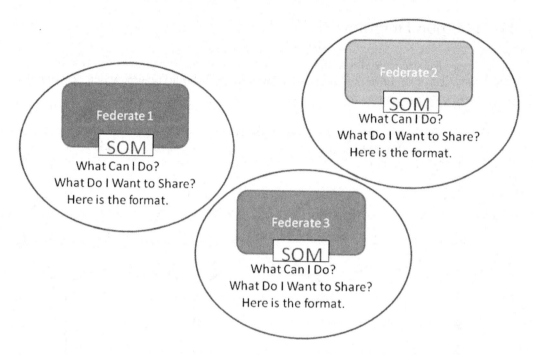

Figure 64. Simulation Object Models.

Federation Object Model

The Federation Object Model (FOM) describes the shared object, attributes and interactions for the whole federation. It is a superset of all SOMs in the federation.

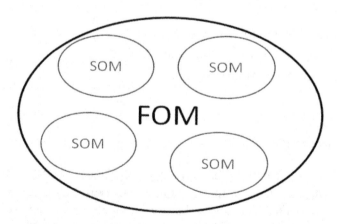

Figure 65. Federation Object Model (FOM).

The bottom-up approach to create a FOM is to aggregate the SOM's representing each federate. The top-down approach is to select a FOM and ensure that each SOM is compliant with it.

RPR-FOM

A typical FOM used in military distributed simulation exercises is the Real-Time Platform-Level Reference FOM (RPR-FOM, pronounced "reaper-fom"). As the name suggests, this is a reference FOM that outlines common military interactions between platforms. The document describing the FOM can be downloaded from the SISO Standards website[27]. It is based upon the IEEE 1278 DIS standard and allows interoperability between DIS simulators and HLA federates. Just to prove that simulationists have a sense of humor, the companion document for the FOM is called the Guidance, Rationale and Interoperability Mappings (to the) RPR-FOM.

The current version of the RPR-FOM is v2.0 draft 17. The document has been stuck at draft 17 for several years and appears that this will be the last version to be implemented.

Management Object Model

The Management Object Model (MOM) is designed to provide management information and control of the RTI, federates and the federation using objects and interactions during runtime. It achieves this using the normal publish and subscribe mechanisms of a federate that is part of the HLA federation.

There are four classes of MOM interactions:

1. Adjust interactions and control of the federation, federate and RTI;
2. Request interactions get RTI information from another federate;
3. Report interactions report RTI data about a federate; and
4. Service interactions are used to invoke RTI services on behalf of another federate.

Typical attributes that the MOM tracks are:

1. Federation Information;
    a. Federation name;
    b. List of federates;

---

[27] http://www.sisostds.org/

      c.   RTI version; and

      d.   Save status.

2. Federate information;

      a.   Federate type and ID;

      b.   Host name of computer;

      c.   Time management information;

      d.   State of the federate;

      e.   Object and interaction information;

            i.   Number of objects and interactions;

           ii.   Number of interactions sent and received;

          iii.   Number of objects updated and reflected;

          iv.   Number of objects owned.

RTI Closer Look

The RTI has three main components. Each of these components interacts with one another in order to create the publish and subscribe mechanism that makes the simulators interoperate. These components are:

1. **RTIExec** (RTI Executive). The RTIExec is a global process that manages the creation and destruction of multiple federation executions. It ensures that each FedExec has a unique name to avoid conflicts on the network. It executes on one platform and listens to a known port;

2. **FedExec** (Federation Executive). There is only one FedExec process per federation. It is created by the first federate to join the federation. The FedExec manages multiple federates joining and leaving the federation execution and facilitates data exchange between federates; and

3. **libRTI** (The RTI Library). The libRTI makes the HLA service methods available to federates. It is normally provided as a C++ or Java interface for applications. Examples of the libRTI that might be found (depending on the HLA RTI used) include libRTI1516.dll and libRTI-NG.dll. A developer, creating a federate for use within an HLA federation, will compile their application with the libRTI of the target HLA RTI and communicate through it to the federation.
Note that libRTI's from different HLA RTI developers are not interoperable (despite being an IEEE standard), if they are 1516-2010 compliant, they *may* use Dynamic Link Compatibility (DLC) to ensure federate compatibility. Refer to the DLC section later in this chapter.

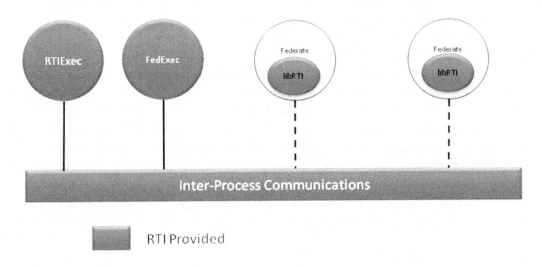

Figure 66. RTI Components.

libRTI and Federate

The diagram below is a conceptual model of an HLA federate showing the relationship between the federate code and the RTI.

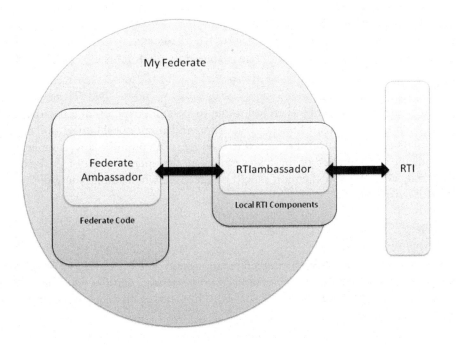

Figure 67. Conceptual Federate Model.

At a very high level, the different components perform the following tasks:

1. **Federate Code**. This provides the functionality of the federate.
2. **Federate Ambassador**. The federate code must implement the FederateAmbassador class that is provided in the libRTI library. This in turn communicates with the RTIAmbassador.
3. **Local RTI Components (LRC)**. The LRC provides the external functionality that is described in the Federate Interface Specification (IEEE 1516.1-2010).
4. **RTIambassador**. This is the federate interface to the RTI. The RTIambassador class interacts with the RTI to initially get the address of the FedExec and allows it to join to and resign from the federation. It also sends all of the data required to allow the federate to interact within the federation.

Federation Configuration Files

Standard federations are able to be reconfigured and re-used for different synthetic environments and distributed simulation events. Rather than hard-code the configuration information within the applications, configuration data is held in separate files that can be changed easily without recompiling source code.

The main configuration files that will be required when an HLA federation is implemented are:

1. Federation Execution Details (FED) File (HLA v1.3 only);
2. FOM Document Data (FDD) File (IEEE 1516); and
3. RTI Initialization Data (RID) File (required for both HLA 1.3 and IEEE 1516 federations).

The configuration of these files is critical to the successful operation of a federation. These files can be the cause of many hours of frustration and are not well understood by many simulation practitioners. Over the years the developers of commercial RTI applications have made the configuration of these files easier and the operation out of the box mostly painless, however care and attention should be exercised when editing these files to ensure successful federation execution.

FED File

The FED file is used in HLA v1.3 implementations and it gives the RTI all of the necessary details it requires to create a new federation. It is in essence a text file (with an extension of *.fed) that is read by the RTI when it is started. This loads in all the required parameters specific to the federation.

It contains information such as routing spaces, objects and interactions to be used during the federation execution. Basically it is a description of the FOM. The FED file was automatically generated from the objects and interactions developed using tools such as the Object Model Development Tool (OMDT) provided free by DMSO. It automated the process of creating the FED file. There is only one FED file per federation.

FDD File

The FDD file is used in IEEE 1516 federations and it performs basically the same function as the legacy FED file by providing the RTI all of the necessary details it requires to create a new federation. It is the data and information contained within a FOM document and is used to initialize the federation execution (FedExec).

In order to support the IEEE 1516 standard, the FDD file must contain the following FOM data tables:

1. Object class structure;
2. Interaction class structure;
3. Attributes;
4. Parameters;
5. Dimension;
6. Transportation type; and
7. Switches.

The FDD is an XML-based file format. There is only one FDD file per federation.

RID File

The RID file is read by the RTI on startup. This supplies user configuration data to the specific RTI used. Typical information contained within a RID file is:

- Log file enabling and level for fault-finding and recording of major RTI events;
- RTI Host IP address and port;
- Multicast endpoint;
- LRC timeout values;
- Federation name (over-ride); and
- Send and receive buffer size values.

There is one RID file per RTI implementation and the type of file varies between RTI vendors. Most use an XML type file structure.

Federate Configuration Files

Configuration files are used so that a federate can be reconfigured for reuse in different federation environments. The files are read by the simulation application at startup to set various parameters. The type and number of federation configuration files depends on the federate itself. There are no particular standards for implementation of these because they are implemented by the developer of the federate and can vary between systems. Typical federate configuration files are:

- LRC network settings (IP address, port);
- Local federate settings (federate name, type, country, forceID etc);
- Enumeration mappings (map models to specific enumerations received); and
- Terrain type and location (latitude and longitude of origin point and map projection used).

Common mistakes made by developers are to have a separate configuration file for each major enumeration type and event. For example, a federate that I worked with had eight separate configuration text files:

1. LRC network settings;
2. Local federate settings;
3. Terrain settings;
4. DIS Enumeration to vehicle models;
5. DIS Enumerations for human models;
6. DIS Enumeration to munition models;
7. DIS Enumeration to effects; and
8. DIS Enumeration to force ID.

Editing these files for each unique federation execution became a problem because not only did multiple files need to be opened in order to make a simple change but each one had the same enumeration listed in different parts of the files. Developers should ensure that configuration files are kept to a minimum and are easy to understand and edit by users.

There are really only two configuration files that are needed for a federate:

1. Local Federate settings.
    a. LRC network settings (IP and port);
    b. Debug options;
    c. Federate name;
    d. Federate (own ship) entity enumeration;
    e. Tick interval;
    f. Lookahead interval;
    g. Time management method; and

      h.   Terrain origin point (with optional height above sea level), latitude and longitude.
3.   DIS Enumeration Mappings;
      a.   Force ID, enumeration = model/effect displayed

The DIS enumeration file can contain the munition enumerations as well. Various types of vehicles and country of origin can be placed into different sections within the file and comment fields can be used as section headers. If developers create these files as XML, then they can easily be read and edited by an application created for that purpose.

HLA Evolved

The IEEE 1516-2010 series of updates was code-named "HLA Evolved" prior to its ratification by IEEE. It introduced a number of important enhancements to the specification to improve performance and extend functionality. Some of these are:

1. **Dynamic Link Compatibility:** That means federates can switch which RTI they use without recompiling/re-linking their application. (Finally! This was always one of the biggest complaints with federate developers.)
2. **Update Rate Reduction:** This new feature allows federates to tell the RTI they can only handle data updates below a certain rate. This allows federates that are update rate constrained to participate in busy federations without bogging down.
3. **Modular FOMs:** Modular FOMs allow federation developers to break up their object model into useful parts. These are called FOM Modules. Each federate only needs to know about the FOM Modules it uses. This is important also when popular FOMs (such as the RPR-FOM) have local extensions. These can now be placed into a FOM Module so that they do not impact upon the core FOM.
4. **WEB Services API (WSDL):** This defines a Web Service Description Language (WSDL) "binding". This is similar to the C++, or Java bindings, but for the Web. The principle is basically the same as for a web server and a web browser. It allows a server on the internet to support HLA based interoperability with clients in different locations.
5. **Fault Tolerance:** The new standard provides a way in which federates can poll the federation to get information into the current state of the federation. This allows federates to know if another federate has dropped off the federation.

Starting a Federation

A recommended sequence for starting an HLA federation is shown in the table below.

Step	User Action	Result
1	A user starts the RTI.	RTIExec launches
2	A user starts a federate.	RTI creates FedExec
3	Other federates join in sequence.	

The sequence should be determined prior to the distributed simulation exercise beginning. Launching the federation in this manor aids in fault finding and ensures that the FedExec has created the federation for the other federates to join. Remember that the first federate to join creates the federation and its name. The most solid federate should be designated as the primary federate to start the federation. Experience will show which one should fulfill this role. You may decide that it is a vehicle simulator, Semi-Automated Forces (SAF), or a Stealth Viewer, it doesn`t matter as long as it is consistent. You may also decide that a specific location will be responsible for creation of the federation due to network bandwidth, or command and control considerations.

Message Order, Timing and Time Advancement

Most federation managers do not necessarily need to know how messages get around the federation in the right order, but there are times when this can become an issue particularly when running distributed simulations over a network between distant locations. Familiarity with the basic concepts can be useful.

Message Timing

Distributed simulation applications interact with messages encapsulated in PDUs as we have described previously. These messages have an associated "time-stamp" and must be delivered to the receiving federate in the correct order with respect to this time-stamp. Such messages are said to be delivered in "Time Stamped Order" (TSO).

Without this timing we might have the unfortunate side-effect of an explosion occurring before we detect that the shot has been fired! A simulation that is publishing its data in TSO can publish in any time order and the RTI will guarantee to deliver the messages in the correct time order.

There are other types of messages that may not have a time stamp associated with it. This might be information type messages. These are delivered on arrival and have no association with the time the message is sent. Messages that are delivered in the order in which they are received are said to be delivered in "Receive Order" (RO).

Time-Constrained and Time-Regulating Federates

The time of each federate must be coordinated with the time of the other federates to guarantee the correct time-ordered delivery of messages. There is a possibility that some federates might finish processing data before others. The time in a federate always moves forward, but the current time in all federates may not be the same. These federates cannot be allowed to advance their time to the next time step before the other federates, so limitations are imposed on this time advance by a federate that receives time stamped data. These federates are said to be "Time Constrained". Federates that publish time-stamped data are known as a "Time Regulating" federate.

For time management services in a federation to control the advancement of time for time constrained federates, the RTI will need to be told when all the publishers of data are finished sending their messages. When this has been completed, the simulation will advance to the next time step.

DIS and HLA RTI Comparison

In the simple example below shown in the table[28], we can see that there is very little difference between DIS and HLA when it comes to interacting within a distributed simulation. The most apparent difference is that DIS sends all of the object attributes (the entity state PDU) when any attribute changes, while the HLA RTI sends only the changes to attributes.

There are also key differences in that the distributed simulation functionality is built into the DIS application (implicit) and in HLA the calls must be made to the RTI (explicit) for requests. For example, an HLA federate must make a request for an object (entity) ID to the RTI and then instantiate the object. In DIS, each simulation assigns object ID's according to an algorithm based on the DIS assigned site number and the host number.

Action	DIS	RTI	Comments
Create an exercise	Define (or use) an exercise ID	Create Federation execution	
Join the exercise	Listen and send PDUs as appropriate	Join Federation Execution	Implicit vs Explicit
Get an object ID (entity)	Application creates a unique ID	Request object ID(s) from the RTI	

---

[28] Table and related information courtesy Mr James O. Calvin, MIT Lincoln Laboratory and Richard Weatherly, Ph.D., The MITRE Corporation, from their paper "An Introduction to the High Level Architecture (HLA) Runtime Infrastructure (RTI)".

Create an object (entity)	Start sending ESPDUs	Instantiate Object	
Discover new object (entity)	ESPDU from unknown entity arrives	Instantiate Discovered Object	Call from RTI to federate software
Tank moves forward	send entity state PDU	Update Attribute Value (position)	RTI sends only the changed data (position)
Tank moves turret	send entity state PDU	Update Attribute Value (turret orientation)	RTI sends only the changed data (turret orientation)
Tank fires at tank	send fire PDU	Send interaction (direct fire)	virtually identical
Delete object (entity)	Stop sending ESPDUs	Delete Object	Implicit vs Explicit
Leave the exercise	Stop listening and sending PDUs	Resign Federation Execution	Implicit vs Explicit
Terminate exercise	All simulations stopped	Destroy Federation Execution	Implicit vs Explicit

Pros and Cons of HLA

The table below shows a high-level summary of the pros and cons of using HLA in a distributed simulation environment when compared to DIS.

Pros	Cons
• Efficient use of bandwidth • FOM is extensible • RTI lets different types of systems interact • Scalable • Can run in real time or slower/faster than real time • Any type of world coordinate system can be used • Web services allow distributed simulation on the Internet	• RTI is complicated to set up and maintain • Standard is often implemented differently across vendors • Relies on large shared state (synthetic environment) • A badly coded federate can bring the whole distributed simulation down • Different RTI's are not compatible • FOM specific tools are required • Commercial RTI licenses and tools are expensive

8 Design and Management of Distributed Simulations

Introduction

In this chapter we explore methodologies for the design and management of a distributed simulation activity. Simulation exercises can be intimidating when starting with a blank sheet of paper and orders from superiors to make it happen. The success or failure of these can come down to the smallest of details and of course unexpected issues that will crop up now and again. Although the later is something that we obviously cannot foresee, having solid fall-back plans and alternative solutions will help in reducing or negating the affects of such problems.

The lifecycle of a distributed simulation activity does not stop with the execution of a synthetic environment. It includes analysis of the data collected in order to provide a set of quantifiable results. These results are used to determine if the initial objectives to run the simulation event have been met or not.

Keep in mind that there are three absolutely critical points to consider when developing distributed simulation environments:

1. Value of the Simulation Investment;
2. Cost of the Simulation Investment; and
3. Risk of the Simulation Investment.

Value of the Simulation Investment

The value (or benefit) of a simulation investment can be determined in many different ways and is going to be dependent upon the desired outcome. For example, is the value going to be determined by one or more of the following factors?

- Number of lives saved;
- Number of training days saved;
- Pedagogical value;
- Will it simplify currently complex processes/systems?
- Money saved;
- Time saved;
- Will enable "xyz equipment" to be used in a distributed simulation for testing in multiple scenarios; and
- Another other factors that are specific to your organization.

Consideration of the value early: particularly during the user needs phase, can lead to more innovative use of the resources assigned to the project and perhaps lead to positive changes of scope. The list above can easily be turned into a series of questions that could be asked in order to derive the value proposition. For example:

- Will the simulation investment save lives?
- Can I save money using the distributed simulation?
- Will I be able to field the equipment sooner if I use simulation?
- Can I use simulation for dangerous conditions that would otherwise put equipment and personnel in life threatening situations?
- Can I incorporate simulation into the actual equipment?
- Can I incorporate simulation into the equipment procurement project?

Cost of the Simulation Investment

The overall cost of the simulation investment could include not only design and development costs, but ongoing maintenance, support and upgrades during its lifecycle. Also consider what the cost will be if it does not go ahead. The overall cost of the simulation investment will be a factor in determining the case for it as well as making decisions on the budgets required.

Risk of the Simulation Investment

There are many types of risk and many articles and books written on risk. The topic is very broad as one could imagine. In order to focus risk in the context of distributed simulation, I tend to look at distributed simulation as relating to and assisting with operational problems. Operational risk is a risk arising from the execution of people, processes and technology in the environment that the organization operates within. This risk also includes physical and environmental risks. Although taken from the definition of risk from the banking industry, it is relevant to discussions of risk associated with distributed simulation:

"Operational risk is the risk of loss resulting from inadequate or failed internal processes, people and systems, or from external events."[29]

The following are examples of general questions that should be asked at the beginning of the simulation project:

- What is the risk if the simulation investment goes ahead?
- What is the risk if the simulation investment does <u>not</u> go ahead?
- What is the risk of the systems involved failing, or not operating correctly?
- What is the risk that we will not have subject matter experts available?
- What is the risk of the network failing?

It might be appropriate to incorporate a risk register or matrix within the project plan in order to properly track and manage the risks associated with the project.

DSEEP, FEDEP and SEDEP

DSEEP, FEDEP and SEDEP are acronyms for processes used to design, implement, execute and test simulation environments. The Distributed Simulation Engineering and Execution Process (DSEEP) will replace IEEE 1516.3 -2003 Federation Development and Execution Process (FEDEP). (The interim reference for the standard is IEEE P1730.) This standard describes a high-level process for developing distributed simulations. FEDEP is tailored for HLA federations and DSEEP is a more generic process for distributed simulation environments.

SEDEP or Synthetic Environment Development and Exploitation Process was an initiative to promote the use of synthetic environments in Europe. It was a complementary process

---

[29] Basel II: International Convergence of Capital Measurement and Capital Standards: a Revised Framework. June 2004.

to the FEDEP and provided an additional step to determine the User Needs. (This has now been included within Step 1 of DSEEP.)

The underlying philosophy in any of these processes is one of re-use of modeling and simulation assets and components.

This chapter will focus on the new DSEEP methodology as a way to design and implement a distributed simulation environment. Note that the methodology is a guide for implementation. It should be tailored to the needs of a specific project. Some steps or resulting products can be left out or modified. Existing software engineering and project management practices are not supplanted by this process, but are easily integrated into the process described here. I have used FEDEP and SEDEP within highly structured software engineering organizations using IEEE standards as well as with Agile software development.

A word of advice is that these processes are oriented towards software and systems engineers, however the majority of distributed simulation projects that I have been involved in have not been run by engineers, but by technical project managers and/or non-technical management. Even the process is described as "..a generic, common-sense systems engineering methodology[30]". In my opinion, the presentation of overly technical engineering processes to non-engineering staff add to the lack of understanding and adoption of these processes by modeling and simulation practitioners.

A wall full of UML diagrams tend to make my eyes glaze over. Simple block diagrams and pictures can be more descriptive when sharing ideas with SME's, equipment operators and other personnel that are involved in distributed simulation events. Technical documents can be shared amongst technical staff, but other products are required for non-technical staff that are part of the exercise. Remember the KISS principle.

Roles

Before delving into each of the steps in more detail, it is important to highlight the roles that generally come into play in distributed simulation planning and execution. These roles are dependent upon the scope of the distributed simulation event and may not be present, or could be held by the same person at different phases of the project.

For planning purposes, assign a person/s or group responsible until the role becomes unnecessary, or is deemed not required. This should be documented in the Distributed Simulation Agreements Document (DSAD), described further in this chapter.

---

[30] RTO-MP-MSG-060. Improving the Federation Agreements Definition – New Proposals Out of the NATO MSG-052 Working Group "Knowledge Network for Federation Architecture and Design". Chaigneau, Cutts and Huiskamp.

Project/SE Manager

The Synthetic Environment (SE) Manager has the primary responsibility for the delivery of the Synthetic Environment. In traditional terms, this is the Project Manager. This person is responsible for the creation and dissemination of the DSAD.

Exercise/Synthetic Environment (or Federation) Controller

The Exercise or Synthetic Environment (or Federation) Controller is the person that controls the execution of the entire Synthetic Environment. There is normally only one SE Controller. This person will start and stop the entire simulation event and ensure that the scenario sequence of events is being followed for the synthetic environment. This could be different individuals particularly if the exercise is a blend of live, constructive and virtual elements in a larger exercise.

Instructor Operator

The Instructor Operator is a person who handles the simulation system hardware and software and controls the execution of the scenario for the local instance of the simulation, or the distributed federation. They start and stop the local simulation environment on cue from the SE Controller. They may also be responsible for injecting faults, hazards or other scenario variables into the environment. There could be multiple Instructor Operators in a distributed simulation.

Simulator Operator

The Simulator Operator is the person that operates the simulator/federate during the exercise, i.e. a pilot or driver. Depending on the type of exercise, the operator roles could be filled by anyone, or qualified and experienced users of that equipment type such as fighter pilots, armored vehicle crew commanders and so on.

Subject Matter Expert (SME)

Subject Matter Experts (SME) may be required to provide insight and specific expertise on any number of topics within the distributed simulation. This could be advice on specific equipment operation, tactics and procedures, industrial processes, weapons parameters and so on.

Terrain/Scenery Builder

The Terrain/Scenery Builder is a person or group who builds, buys and/or collates the terrain required for the different simulators in the exercise.

3D Model Builder/Artist

The 3D Model Builder or Artist is a person or group who builds, buys and/or collates the 3D models required for the different simulators in the exercise.

Simulation Developer

A Developer is a person who develops the simulators, federates or other software assets required for use within the synthetic environment.

Network Engineer

The Network Engineer is responsible for planning and implementing the network infrastructure and bandwidth required to run the distributed simulation. During execution, they are responsible for ensuring that the network is maintained and operational in accordance with the specifications required.

Test and Validation

The Test and Validation person is responsible for the Proof of Compliance Plan Testing to ensure that the correct data is being collected for analysis and validation.

Observer

The Observer is the generally a stakeholder representative that has oversight to the project to ensure the requirements and objectives for the project are being met.

Logistics and Maintenance Support

The logistics support specialist is responsible for oversight of the logistics and maintenance requirements for the distributed simulation environment. For larger programs, there may be a requirement to generate a bill of materials (BOM), asset catalog and other documents and coordinate maintenance support before, during and after the distributed simulation event has been completed.

DSEEP Overview

DSEEP[31] is a seven step process which defines the entire lifecycle of a modeling and simulation application from initial conception through to the analysis of results. Each of the steps is further divided into Activities/sub-steps.

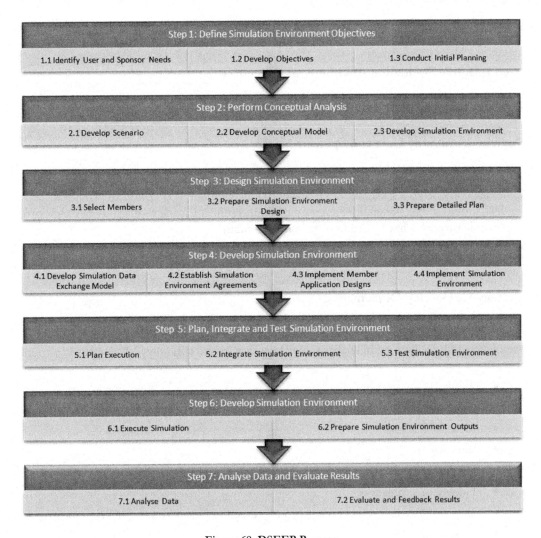

Figure 68. DSEEP Process.

---

[31] As described on the SISO standards website.

The process itself is just a guide, not a template. It does not define the outputs required for each step in specific terms because it is an overlay onto any existing software engineering and/or project management process that might be used in your own organization. The products that are generated at each step may be tailored to different audiences as required. I have suggested some general outputs for each step based on a simple distributed simulation exercise environment for consideration.

Step 1: Define Simulation Environment Objectives

This step is broken down into three activities:

Activity 1.1 Identify User and Sponsor Needs

The requirement to build a distributed simulation comes from a specific need. These needs generally come from a stakeholder, or group of stakeholders. It is critical to provide a clear understanding of the stakeholder's requirement and reflect it back to them to gain sign-off. The whole project is likely based on this understanding.

Output: A User Needs document.

Activity 1.2 Develop Objectives

A detailed set of specific objectives are developed and documented. The capability of the simulation to be able to address these objectives is assessed and considered against:

- Value;
- Cost;
- Risks;
- Timescales;
- Personnel availability;
- Fidelity of simulation;
- Test and Validation (i.e. how do you foresee the objective success being measured);
- Supporting tools;
- Security;
- Interoperability;
- Network Constraints;
- Geographic dispersal;
- Facilities; and

- Potential solution approaches/options.

Potential Output: Depending on the development process used, this could be an updated User Needs document to keep it simple, or a separate document that specifies the objectives for the simulation event.

Activity 1.3 Conduct Initial Planning

Initial planning documentation is produced that provides the initial project execution plan (i.e. a Gantt chart with high-level milestones) as well as items such as plans for configuration management, quality assurance, (including Validation, Verification (V&V)), security, risk mitigation and so on.

Potential Outputs: Project Plan and Project Execution Plan documents.

Step 2: Perform Conceptual Analysis

This step is broken down into three activities.

Activity 2.1 Develop Scenario

The objectives identified in Step 1 are assessed in terms of how they might be represented in the real world and from this a prototype scenario is developed. Several vignettes may be produced in order to fully satisfy the objectives. Scenario information should include the number and types of all the main entities, their positions, capabilities and behavior and scenario exit criteria. Geographical location and environmental conditions should also be specified. Potential reuse of previously established scenarios should be considered.

I tend to use Google Earth or Bing Maps to develop scenarios and plan the sequences of events that make up a vignette on geography that the simulation is to be conducted on. Even better (if you can get it) is recent aerial imagery and photographs of the area. This will ensure that distinctive features are seen and possibly incorporated into the scenario.

The use of simple scenario conceptual diagrams (also known as Rich Pictures) will also assist in the dissemination and understanding of the scenario. The following diagrams were used in one exercise to describe the high-level interactions required to fulfill the objectives of the distributed simulation. The objectives were to integrate two disparate simulation systems on a DIS network and have each one see and interact with entities being injected into the synthetic environment. Two vignettes were used to illustrate this interaction and prove the objective. The first was to have Simulator 1 provide a convoy of trucks driving along a road and Simulator 2 provide a column of tanks passing the trucks. Simulator 2 also provided a UAV to circle over the event. The second vignette provided a fire and detonation event interaction. The trucks from Simulator 1 were replaced with an enemy tank and the simulators engaged each other.

UAV Simulator 2

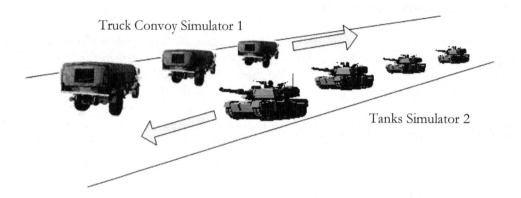

Truck Convoy Simulator 1

Tanks Simulator 2

Vignette 1 Conceptual Diagram: Convoys from two simulators pass each other.

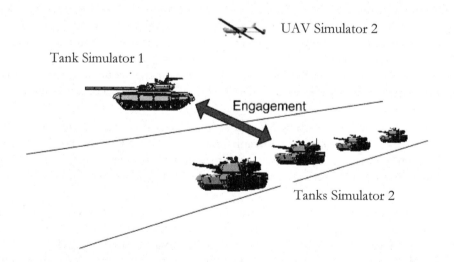

UAV Simulator 2

Tank Simulator 1

Engagement

Tanks Simulator 2

Vignette 2 Conceptual Diagram: Tanks from two simulators engage each other.

I will then use an excel spreadsheet to record and describe the sequence of events and put them onto a timeline. This is called the Master Sequence of Events List (MSEL). This can also be used during the execution of the distributed simulation to ensure that events are being injected appropriately into the scenario when required.

A secondary benefit is that while planning the event, you should become very familiar with the terrain and scenery that the simulation is to be conducted over. Watch out for terrain elevation data mismatches however. The flat land that you thought was a park in Google Earth, could easily be a hill in the terrain that has been built and delivered to you for the exercise using higher fidelity terrain source data. The sudden appearance of a massive hill in your carefully planned scenario might be problematic later on. (Again, ask me how I know this!)

The following should also be considered and documented:

1.   Operational Environment;
     a.   Types and numbers of entities that are to be represented in the distributed simulation;
     b.   Description of the capabilities of the entities, their behavior and the relationships and interactions between them; and
     c.   Initial conditions, behavior, interactions, timelines and so on for each entity.
2.   Natural Environment;
     a.   Geographic region;
     b.   Specific elements of interest. For example man-made and natural features (hills, railway lines, roads, buildings etc);
     c.   Tidal conditions;
     d.   Moon state;
     e.   Time of day/year; and
     f.   Weather.

Potential Outputs:

- Initial Master Sequence of Events List (MSEL);
- Scenario description with imagery, maps and conceptual models.

Activity 2.2 Develop Conceptual Model

From the scenario, the conceptual model can be established and documented if it is required. This is a real world representation that is independent of any implementation. This step transforms the original objectives into a set of functional and behavioral descriptions designed to meet them.

The term "conceptual model" is defined as:

> 'the conceptual model is a non-software specific description of the computer simulation model (that will be, is or has been developed), describing the objectives, inputs, outputs, content, assumptions and simplifications of the model'[32]

Conceptual models are used to help us understand the subject matter they represent. They can be a representation of a physical object, such as a car and perhaps the associated processes required to refuel it, through to an abstract mathematical model. The model may represent a single thing, such as a Chevrolet truck, or a class of things, such as all trucks.

From this conceptual model, we might decide that within our scenario, it will be important to represent certain real-world activities with a higher fidelity than others. For example, in our convoy scenarios described previously, we may decide that the ground physics modeling of the vehicles travelling across the terrain is not as important as the ballistics models of the weapons.

In SEDEP, the federation conceptual model is defined using UML, or similar modeling tool. It may be the approach that DSEEP takes as well once it is ratified as a standard. A non-technical audience, faced with a wall covered in UML diagrams, will soon lose interest, so my advice is to keep the UML to developer audiences and use Rich Diagrams and other diagrammatic ways of showing the conceptual model. The Department of Defense Architectural Framework (DoDAF) uses "All View" (AV), which I have used in the past to represent a simulation conceptual model at a high level. DoDAF is another process that can be used in conjunction with DSEEP (it falls outside the scope of this book; however I have used it successfully within a major simulation project to provide documentation of tasks and activities required to fulfill stakeholder objectives.)

The NATO Modelling and Simulation Group (MSG) suggest the creation of the conceptual model will take into account the following[33];

- **Conceptual interplay**: this is an abstraction of the potential relation between conceptual entities. Many of the BOM (Base Object Model) concepts could be applied here.
- **Conceptual entity**: This is a type of instance. It is defined by an entity's capabilities and the conceptual interplays which could be managed.

---

[32] Robinson, S. 2008. Conceptual modelling for simulation part I: definition and requirements. *Journal of the Operational Research Society* 59 (3): 278-290.
[33] NATO document MP-MSG-062-02, "Improving the Federation Agreements Definition – New Proposals Out of the NATO MSG-052 Working Group "Knowledge Network or Federation Architecture and Design", Chaigneau, Cutts and Huiskamp.

- **Capability**: The potential ability to do work, perform a function or mission, achieve an objective, or provide a service.
- **Capability ontology**: to manage an accredited vocabulary corresponding to the metadata "capability" in the specific context.
- **Cooperation**: conceptual interplay sent in cooperation with other conceptual entities (for instance a network message). This kind of interplay has to know his destination (e.g. used to model an operational network).
- **Blind interplay**: conceptual interplay sent without knowing targets (for instance detonation interplays). This kind of interplay doesn't need to know to which it has been sent. Used to model physical phenomena like detections, detonations, …
- **Aggregate**: this conceptual interplay expresses a link of composition between two conceptual entities (e.g.an aircraft and one of its component radar). The link between the two elements is permanent in the context the simulation.
- **Affiliation:** this conceptual interplay is a link of aggregation between two conceptual entities (e.g. an aircraft and a missile). In the context of the simulation, the two elements could have different relationship during the scenario.

The FEDEP and SEDEP provide a list of suggested tasks when developing a Conceptual Model that are relevant to this DSEEP activity. I have taken out specific references to Federations in order to generalize them and provide them here as a prompt for ideas on things to think about when you are looking to develop your own conceptual model:

- Agree on a Conceptual Model format and means of documentation;
- Analyze the source information for this activity – i.e. Scenario Requirements, User Requirements, Evaluation Objectives, and Evaluation Definition;
- Check for re-usable (parts of) existing models;
- Identify all relevant major elements in the distributed simulation;
- Identify generalizations and specializations of already identified elements as needed;
- Identify parts of already identified elements as needed;
- Specify all relevant structural relationships between the identified elements;
- Identify all data that needs to be dynamically exchanged between identified elements;
- Specify auxiliary data types for data as needed;
- Specify dynamic relationships for all dynamic data exchanges between the involved elements;
- Specify behavioral aspects of the elements, especially those involving dynamic data exchange (sequence, processing, transformation, etc.);
- Specify attributes of elements as appropriate;

- Specify transformational aspects (functions) of elements as appropriate;
- Specify traceability information;
- Document an explanatory listing of assumptions, limitations, and specification decisions;
- Document references to relevant authoritative resources;
- Document a dictionary, ontology, or other suitable description as appropriate;
- Iterate until the Conceptual Model stabilizes;
- Verify for completeness, consistency, accuracy, and required amount of detail;
- Correct issues found during verification and re-verify;
- Validate with all stakeholders; and
- Correct issues found during validation, re-verify, and re-validate. This may involve corrections needed outside the Conceptual Model.

Activity 2.3 Develop Simulation Environment Requirements

The detailed requirements for the simulation are established from the conceptual model. (If a conceptual model was not considered, then it is derived from the scenario.) These requirements are also extended to consider the following simulation environment specific issues such as;

- Exercise control;
- Monitoring;
- Data logging and analysis;
- Networks;
- Test Criteria; and
- Initial Personnel requirements.

In this activity, you should consider the following;

- Agree on the System Requirements format, use of standardized templates and means of documentation. This will vary in accordance with the systems engineering processes that are used in your organization. It may be that the sponsor organization will mandate the formats and standard to be used;
- Analyze source information for this activity, i.e. Scenario, User Requirements, Evaluation Objectives, and Evaluation Definition;
- Specify one or more system requirements for each user requirement that cannot be covered by the Conceptual Model. Consider amongst others the following;

- o   Required characteristics, behaviors, constraints of simulation elements or data specified in the Conceptual Model;
- o   Requirements for live, virtual, constructive simulation;
- o   Fidelity requirements of simulation elements;
- o   Performance requirements;
- o   Time management requirements e.g. real-time versus slower or faster than real-time;
- o   Computer and networking requirements;
- o   Supporting software requirements;
- o   Security requirements for personnel, hardware, network data and software.
- o   Execution management requirements;
- o   System requirements for supporting evaluation e.g. data loggers, data analysis software etc;
- o   Simulation operation personnel requirements; and
- o   Simulation operation training requirements.

- For each system requirement decide on the best language to use;
- Specify each system requirement using the selected language and define a verification method;
- If a system requirement is to be verified using automated testing, define one or more test cases;
- Specify traceability information for each system requirement;
- Document an explanatory listing of assumptions, limitations, and specification decisions;
- Document references to relevant authoritative resources;
- Document a dictionary, ontology, or other suitable description as appropriate;
- Iterate until the System Requirements stabilize;
- Verify each system requirement using the defined verification method;
- Correct issues found during verification and re-verify;
- Validate with all stakeholders; and
- Correct issues found during validation, re-verify, and re-validate. This may involve corrections needed outside the System Requirements.

Potential Output:

- At this stage it will be appropriate to put together the initial draft of the Distributed Simulation Agreements Document (DSAD) in the format that has been agreed. It will include placeholders for data and agreements to come. A sample template is provided at Appendix A of this book.

Step 3: Design Simulation Environment

This step is broken down into three activities.

Activity 3.1 Select Members

Components of the Simulation Environment (known within DSEEP as 'members') are selected, and may vary in size from small elements to complete simulation environments in themselves. It is important to determine if pre-existing members can be reused (with the aid of a repository, if available), and to what extent, they may need to be modified. Rationale for member selection should be documented.

Identify and assess:

- Suitable distributed simulation environments;
- Suitable simulators/federates;
- Suitable components;
- Suitable databases (including terrain);
- Suitable runtime management tools;
- Suitable After Action and Review (AAR) tools; and
- Suitable network components.

A point to note that when selecting members, ensure that the licensing agreements are in line with the intended use. Some simulation assets are very specific in usage rights and the fact that they have been used in a project before, does not mean that they can be used again in your project.

Activity 3.2 Prepare Simulation Environment Design

The design of new members will need to be established and the complete simulation environment design should be documented, including its overall infrastructure and selection of protocol standards.

When you are designing the simulation environment, consideration should be given to the following:

- Establish approach to be used – e.g., re-use or modify an existing simulation environment or design from scratch;
- Specify interoperability protocol e.g. DIS, HLA, etc;
- Map entities and main functionality onto simulation elements or members;
- Determine approach for updating objects e.g. when parameters change, on a periodic basis, etc;

- Generate simulation environment high-level design and produce a System Design Document;
- Specify high-level design of all simulation environment elements – e.g. network infrastructure, simulators/federates, databases, runtime tools etc;
- Consider security issues;
- Identify additional support tools;
- Specification of buildings/rooms for hosting the distributed simulation e.g. network connects, telephone sockets, power outlets, desks etc;
- Specify network topology;
- Specification of network elements e.g. hubs, routers, gateways, bridges etc;
- Allocation of simulators/members/federates to computers;
- Specification of the computers to be used and their addresses on the network; and
- Specify runtime infrastructure.

Potential Outputs:

- There may be a requirement to produce design documents for different parts of the design. For example terrain databases and network infrastructures. Other documents that may be required could include software user manuals and operations procedures manuals; and
- Iterate DSAD as required.

Activity 3.3 Prepare Detailed Plan

A detailed plan for the established design is put in place. This involves updating and extending the initial Project Plan and Project Execution Plan documentation put in place in Step 1.

The detailed plan should include a comprehensive test plan. In some projects a Proof of Compliance Plan (PCOP) may be required to ensure that the simulation environment is contractually meeting its deliverable obligations to agreed specification.

The test plan may include some, or all, of the following elements:

- Test schedule;
- Test descriptions;
- Compliancy tests;
- Interoperability tests;
- Latency tests;
- Performance tests;
- Functional tests;

- Initialization tests;
- Configuration tests;
- Scenario tests;
- Data collection tests;
- Reliability/robustness tests; and
- Test procedures.

Potential Output:

- Detailed planning documents are produced as required and described in this activity. They will vary according to the project requirements.

Step 4: Develop Simulation Environment

This step contains three activities.

Activity 4.1 Develop Simulation Data Exchange Model

The information exchange data model defines how members within the simulation environment will interact with each other at runtime. The data exchange model should be fully documented, and must conform to the conceptual model established in Step 2.

The information exchange data model may define the following:

- Byte ordering;
- Encoding/decoding scheme;
- Byte boundary alignment for complex data types;
- Dead Reckoning algorithms;
- Approach for object attribute consistency for late joining federates in an HLA federation; and
- Other data that is common in the simulation environment.

Activity 4.2 Establish Simulation Environment Agreements

This activity is designed to ensure that all other agreements relating to interoperation are fully established before the simulation is implemented. Issues to be considered include:

- The need for any further software modifications to pre-existing members;
- The need to ensure database and algorithm consistency, where appropriate;

- Identification of definitive data sources for members and simulation environment databases:
  - database agreements will include details such as size, resolution, level of detail and main features;
- Runtime management agreements, synchronization points and initialization procedures (Start/Stop/Pause);
- The definition of a save and restore strategy;
- The definition of security procedures;
- Data Publication and subscription responsibilities;
- Scenario instances required;
- Time management (real-time or logical time, time evolution and so on); and
- Agreements on simulation-wide algorithms:
  - Detection;
  - Probability of kill;
  - Attrition;
  - Communication delays;
  - Earth projection used;
  - Coordinate system;
  - Units of measurement (e.g. imperial, metric etc)

Potential Outputs:

- Iterate DSAD as required; and
- Update project planning documents as required.

Activity 4.3 Implement Member Application Designs

During this activity, existing members are modified and member interfaces are constructed, adapted or extended as necessary. New members are implemented along with supporting databases and scenario instances.

Activity 4.4 Implement Simulation Environment Infrastructure

At this point, the required network software and hardware infrastructures are created and configured, and the facilities required to support integration and test are fully prepared. This includes availability of hardware, system administration, building air conditioning and power supply, and all other software and hardware configuration necessary. Ensure that security procedures and protocols, if they are required, are in place and understood. The infrastructures should be fully tested before going on to the next step.

It has been my experience that it will be important to continue to take notes of problems and issues encountered (during this activity and moving into the next steps) and the various ways in which these issues were dealt with, or mitigated. This helps to reduce issues in subsequent distributed simulation activities and also helps if you need to produce a post-exercise report or brief a lot more easily!

Examples of some problems that I have encountered during the infrastructure implementation phase have included:

- Not having the right outlet plugs on rack power supplies;
- Not calculating the heat generated by computer racks and having to upgrade simulator room air conditioning units;
- Supplier problems and shipping delays with network hardware;
- Supplier issues for equipment requiring different country voltages (and outlet plugs!);
- Having to testing network infrastructure at off-peak times instead of during normal business hours;
- Approval delays for IT network changes;
- Access approvals for military bases and facilities; and
- Security approvals for room changes.

Potential Outputs:

- Iterate DSAD as required;
- Update project planning documents as required; and
- Potentially require work orders, change requests, visit clearance requests and so on.

Step 5: Plan, Integrate and Test Simulation Environment

This step is broken down into three activities.

Activity 5.1 Plan Execution

The Project Plan and Project Execution Plan should be updated to take into account all the latest developments, paying particular attention to addressing of V&V, test and security issues. All risks and mitigation strategies should be reassessed, and plans for the detailed execution of the simulation fully documented.

Potential Outputs:

- Iterate DSAD as required; and

- Update project planning documents as required.

Activity 5.2 Integrate Simulation Environment

The purpose of this task is to incorporate all members into their intended locations within the simulation environment infrastructure. Detailed progressive testing should be carried out during this process in accordance with the Project Plan and Project Execution Plan and software problems encountered should be fixed and retested.

The following tasks should be undertaken as required:

- Check again that the appropriate hardware is available in each facility;
- Install simulation hardware at each facility/location as required;
- Get simulation environment configuration information;
- Ensure that all necessary software – e.g. HLA RTI, is installed on each host and on each simulator/member/ federate;
- Get network configuration information;
- Configure network components to ensure network connectivity between sites and between hosts; and
- Test network connectivity.

Activity 5.3 Test Simulation Environment

The fully integrated simulation environment is formally tested to ensure that it can meet all its specified objectives. Test results should be reviewed with both users and sponsors, and any necessary corrective actions carried out.

The following tasks should be undertaken as required:

- Run integration tests and document results;
- Perform system-wide tests and document results;
- Demonstrate that the scenario can be performed at the required level of fidelity;
- Demonstrate verification of system requirements; and
- Demonstrate validation of user requirements.

Step 6: Execute Simulation Environment and Prepare Outputs

This step consists of two activities.

Activity 6.1 Execute Simulation

All planned simulation executions take place in accordance with the Project Plan and all raw data outputs are collected. Any problems will be documented.

Preparations for this activity may include training the instructors, operators and technicians participating in the distributed simulation activity and rehearsing the simulation execution to identify unforeseen problems. Depending on the requirements, it may be necessary to perform several simulation executions either using the same scenario, or with a modified scenario.

Tasks could include:

- Preparation:
    - Brief all participants;
    - Configure and initialize simulation environment for a particular scenario;
    - Launch simulation environment;
    - Rehearse scenario; and
    - Verify data collection process.
- Execute Simulation:
    - Launch simulation environment;
    - Execute scenario;
    - Check data has recorded correctly; and
    - Determine if additional execution runs are required.

Activity 6.2 Prepare Simulation Environment Outputs

Any pre-processing that is required to be carried out on the raw execution data outputs now takes place to ensure that it is in the appropriate format for subsequent analysis. This data, along with any execution problems encountered, should be reviewed to assess if there may be a need to rerun some of the simulation executions.

Step 7: Analyze Data and Evaluate Results

There are two activities in this step.

Activity 7.1 Analyze Data

The processed data from Step 6 is analyzed using appropriate tools and methods, and results prepared for feedback to the user or sponsor.

Activity 7.2 Evaluate and Feedback Results

The results are fed back to the User or Sponsor for evaluation, and an assessment made that the objectives of the Simulation Environment have been met. Those products developed or modified during the development process should be archived for subsequent re-use where appropriate. Lessons learned should be captured, and a final report produced.

Tasks to consider during this activity include:

- Evaluate analyzed data;
- Infer conclusions;
- Identify deficiencies and propose corrective actions;
- Identify future work;
- Evaluate how well the simulation environment met user needs;
- Identify lessons learnt;
- Document results and produce a report; and
- Archive all products for potential re-use.

Potential Outputs:

- Evaluation Results Report;
- Lessons Learned Report;
- Final Report; and
- Project close-out documentation.

9   Common DS Implementation Issues

Introduction

There are many things that can go wrong when you are implementing a distributed simulation environment. This chapter is a compilation of various issues that could present themselves at various stages of the design and implementation. Note that this is not an exhaustive list, but some of the more common ones that I have observed, or have learned from. Issues mentioned in previous chapters are repeated here so that they are listed in one place for review prior to implementing your specific distributed simulation environment.

The simulation issues discussed in this chapter are:

- Terrain;
- Models;
- Asset Management;
- License Management;
- Network, Bandwidth and IT;
- Combining DIS and HLA;
- Training;
- Data;
- Configuration;
- Forgetting Logistics;
- Documentation; and
- Project.

Terrain

As mentioned in Chapter 5, this will most likely be the biggest issue that will need to be addressed, particularly if you have different types of simulator within your distributed simulation environment. Even if you are using the same simulation software in each of your simulators, terrain could still present an issue if you do not have the right type of terrain, is not of high-enough fidelity, or is out of date. Review Chapter 5 again prior to discussing terrain options with the project team to make sure the issues are understood.

Common mistakes with terrain are:

- Not allowing enough lead-time for terrain to be built, or procured;
- Wanting to have a very large terrain implemented for your exercise that the simulators will not be able to process;
- Assuming that because the same simulation software is being used, that they have the same terrain. They may actually have different versions of the same terrain;
- Assuming that all simulators will be able to use OpenFlight compiled format;
- Assuming that the terrain will be delivered with different seasons, time of day, or sensor capability (material encoded); and
- Not considering cultural or vegetation requirements specific to the terrain region (i.e. palm trees for the tropics, adobe huts for parts of Africa etc).

Models

The following are common issues faced with 3D models for distributed simulation environments:

- Polygon counts are too high for good performance;
- Polygon counts are too low and make the model unrecognizable;
- Models that do not have Levels of Detail (LOD), or too few LOD nodes;
- Sensor effects are not modeled (either material encoded, or texture swaps);
- Destruction or destroyed states are not modeled;
- Models are not the same in each simulator:
  - The models have different markings (such as different camouflage, or different unit numbers);
  - The models are different versions of the same make (a double-cab pick-up truck instead of a single-cab pick-up, or a T-72 instead of a T-80);
  - The models are a different color (in one exercise scenario, the bad guys are supposed to drive away in a red car, one simulator only had white cars); and

- Vehicles do not have virtual cockpits or panels, only external models. (Some simulation systems, particularly desktop simulators, allow users to drive or fly vehicles and see them from the outside as well as from inside the vehicle.).

Asset Management

As the distributed simulation exercise being planned grows, various assets and resources will be gathered in order to support it. This will include models, terrain, applications, planning tools, documents and so on.

Common issues with distributed simulation assets are:

- Version control. Newer versions of assets are available, but not all owners of simulation applications get them, or know about them. Examples can include:
  - o Simulation applications from software development companies. (I have had companies release four new versions of their software in one six month project timeframe);
  - o Terrain updates;
  - o Model updates;
  - o Documentation updates.
- Distribution of large files. Mechanisms may need to be implemented to distribute very large files, some of which may be many gigabytes in size. (It may be more expedient to ship entire hard drives to users); and
- Classification of assets. Some simulation assets may be classified whilst others are unclassified. These will require different storage, distribution and runtime security measures.

Resource Repository

Keeping track of all of these will be very important, particularly as new or alternative versions of these assets become available. Assets and resources that are used within the distributed simulation environment could be stored in a centralized repository or library for re-use and easy access. Some organizations call this a Modeling and Simulation Resource Repository (MSRR), or a Simulation Resource Library (SRL). It could be a shared drive on a network, a database application, or a web-based library. If the resource itself is not able to be stored in a repository, then the contact details and other information on how to obtain it can be.

It is important that all of the resources that are required are properly accounted for and that the correct versions and location of these resources are also known. Appropriate meta-data should be attached to each resource in order for users to determine if it will meet their needs. This meta-data could include:

- Version number;
- Owner;
- Contact details;
- Description;
- Resource Type (i.e. model, terrain, virtual simulator etc);
- Security Classification; and
- VV&A Comments:
  - Level of VV&A performed; and
  - Suitability for use.

License Management

It is highly likely that the software license for the critical piece of simulation software that you need for the distributed simulation exercise will expire approximately five minutes before you are about to do the first run in front of the Sponsor/General/VIP.

It is an unfortunate reality that software companies in the defense and aerospace industry, believe in renting their software to you, rather than allowing you to purchase it and use it as you see fit. Typical licenses for image generators, HLA RTI's, data loggers, modeling software and so on are for 12 months only and will become inoperative after that period. Some flight simulators may have over a dozen software applications in them and each may have different expiry dates. If you are running a large distributed simulation environment, a way of tracking licenses is critical. It can easily be a full-time role for someone to track and manage these. In addition, each of these software applications may have newer versions that might need to be updated and managed.

A useful tip: A cross platform data-center applications such as Microsoft Systems Center Operations Manager and Configuration Manager can be deployed within the simulation environment to keep an eye on licenses and configurations. It can also be used to push out application updates onto specific Unix or Windows-based computers.

Network, Bandwidth and IT

Distributed simulation environments exist on a network and without a solid infrastructure, the environment will be prone to failure, or at the very least have performance issues. A complete run-down of networking environments and issues is outside the scope of this book. Although it isn't necessary to be a network or IT engineer to implement a basic infrastructure, having an engineer on staff for more than basic environments will be a very good idea. Include a staff position for this task in your project plan if possible.

Network elements typically include routers, switches, hosts and transmission media. There can be multiple networks involved in a distributed simulation and spread geographically around the country, or world. Each one of these elements, like ice on a wing of a plane, introduces drag and inefficiencies as data flows through or across them. Typically we aim for a maximum of 100 milliseconds latency (or delay) from when we send data to when we receive data at the other end (200 milliseconds round-trip). Anything more than that becomes very noticeable as entities in our simulation environment start jumping around and can affect the outcome of our simulation event. In tightly coupled simulation environments, such as a missile and aircraft, or two high-performance jets, the maximum acceptable latency is generally 100 milliseconds between any two hosts.

A router could introduce 10 - 100 milliseconds of delay on a data packet. In a complex network, a typical packet will be forwarded over many links via many gateways or routers, each of which will not begin to forward the packet until it has been completely received. In such an example, the minimal latency is the sum of the latency of each link, plus the forwarding delay of that link, plus the transmission time between each link. When designing a network, equipment that is placed between simulators should be kept to a minimum. The use of frame relay clouds between simulators is not a good idea. Frame relay clouds handle the transmission of packets over a frequently-changing pathway. There are no fixed transmission paths so there is no control over latency.

Bandwidth is technically defined as the amount of information that can flow through a network at a given period of time. This is a theoretical number though and causes a lot of confusion. Just look at your next bill from your internet provider. The bandwidth that you pay for is most likely not what you get to your computer. The actual bandwidth that is available to a certain device on a network is referred to as "throughput".

The protocols that are used within a distributed simulation environment will have an effect on the throughput available. In chapter 3 we discussed that DIS is a broadcast protocol that uses a lot of bandwidth, while HLA is a multicast protocol, which uses less. A direct comparison between DIS and HLA is a little misleading however, the design of the distributed simulation environment itself has a direct bearing on the bandwidth consumption as much as the protocol chosen. A poorly implemented HLA federation might be more of a bandwidth hog than a DIS simulation. The more interactions required between the entities within a simulation, the more bandwidth is consumed. The upper limits in performance will most likely be hit due to the number of entity updates rather than the number of entities themselves.

Many simulation environments are a blend of DIS and HLA. If this is the case, DIS simulation resources should be segregated on their own networks, with single gateways to HLA federations employed where necessary. There may be other applications outside of the simulation environment that also cause available bandwidth to be eaten up. If the network is shared with other resources, such as Voice Over Internet Protocol (VOIP) systems, or internet and office productivity applications, bandwidth for your distributed simulation environment could become problematic.

I was involved with a simulation exercise conducted as a milestone demonstration for a military customer and it was decided to link the simulators located at different military bases together with an IP-based video link. The intent was to provide visiting VIPs with an overview of the exercise showing the remote locations and the simulators being used. We had a dedicated simulation Wide Area Network and tested all simulators running at the same time with the maximum number of entities required for our scenario also sending updates over the network. We ran up the video links between each site and verified that our previous calculation on bandwidth consumption was valid and that there was enough overall bandwidth for our needs. Or so we thought. Unfortunately when the scenario was run properly for the first time, our throughput dropped dramatically and we had to switch off the video feeds completely. We had failed to account for the HLA radio traffic that spiked during a simulated missile engagement. This upsurge in traffic congestion affected the overall network performance. We had calculated the HLA radio traffic for normal operation during the scenario, but had failed to account for the crew intercom traffic within the simulator, which was also on the same HLA radio network.

Do not underestimate the IT expertise that will be required in order to design, implement and manage the distributed simulation environment infrastructure and bandwidth required. There are some simulation specific knowledge requirements that the IT staff should become familiar with in order to assist with creating the distributed simulation environment. This will include understanding the type and amount of traffic that will be on the network, DNS configuration, latency, security requirements, broadcast and multicast components, data capture and analysis and so on. Quality of Service (QoS) is a buzzword that IT folks like to use. This relates to the ability to provide different priority to different applications, users or data flows, or to guarantee a certain level of performance to a data flow. In order for it to work, every hardware component and operating system between the sender and the receiver must support QoS.

A best-effort network or service (as most distributed simulation environments are) does not support quality of service. The alternative to QoS control mechanisms is to provide high quality communication over a best-effort network by over-provisioning the capacity so that it is sufficient for the expected peak traffic load. The resulting lack of traffic congestion caused by the over-provisioning negates the need for QoS mechanisms.

Useful Tips:

- Use a Router/Latency Generator to simulate the introduction of latency, bandwidth restrictions and packet loss when planning complex distributed simulation environments. This will give you an idea of performance issues that may be encountered and whether these will affect the desired outcome of your system. For strategic and operational level scenarios, including humanitarian and emergency responses, homeland security vignettes, military and so on, this may provide a realistic snapshot of actual operational conditions, or the delays of a second or two on the network may not be important to the type of data that is transmitted. One such (open source) application is called Dummynet and is available from the following website; http://info.iet.unipi.it/~luigi/dummynet

- Use a network analysis tool to look at traffic throughput and determine the content of the protocol traffic being sent. One such valuable open source tool is called Wireshark. It can analyze many common traffic protocols including DIS and CIGI (and HLA with user configured data capture). I have used it many times to troubleshoot problems within distributed simulation environments. The ability to look at header information for DIS in particular has led to immediate discovery of problem areas such as protocol version issues and delinquent PDUs causing issues. It can be downloaded from; http://www.wireshark.org

- Ensure that sub-net masking is used to segregate networks from each other in your distributed simulation environment. By organizing hosts into logical groups subnetting can improve network security and performance. The ability to filter traffic between subnets can make more bandwidth available to application and can limit access in desirable ways. As an example, you can have multiple DIS and HLA simulation environments running on the same network if they are segregated using subnet masks.

Combining DIS and HLA

There are times when we will need to combine DIS based simulations with HLA Federations so that these legacy systems can be part of the HLA exercise. In order to do this, we will need to use a DIS Gateway federate in our HLA federation. This is an application that translates DIS PDUs into HLA and vice versa.

Also note that the FOM used within the HLA federation must be based upon RPR-FOM. This is the FOM that is compatible with DIS. Use RPR-FOM 1.0 for DIS version 1 to 5 (IEEE 1278.1 (1992 - 1995)) and RPR-FOM 2.0 draft 17 for DIS version 6 (IEEE 1278.1 (1998)).

Other ways to combine DIS with HLA are to develop your own middleware application to translate the PDUs, or to recode the DIS simulator and integrate into HLA. There are some DIS and HLA middleware libraries available for developers to do this. Be aware that DIS Gateways can be relatively expensive, so try to combine all DIS assets into one network area and use a single gateway to translate to and from an HLA federation environment.

Training

Do not neglect the training component when planning a distributed simulation environment or exercise. There are many common training issues that may be experienced include:

- Assuming that equipment operators are familiar with the specific type of vehicle or system that you are simulating. Your simulator may have an older or newer version of a piece of hardware or software in it that may require operator training prior to using it;
- Software developers may need to be sent on specialized training courses in order to use applications needed to build your simulator or simulation environment;
- Software developers may not know how to operate the simulation environment and may make dangerous assumptions when they are coding applications that will function within the environment. Consider sending developers when planning to run training courses on the operation of existing simulation equipment or environments;
- Assuming that project staff at all levels has distributed simulation, DIS and/or HLA knowledge. Experience with distributed simulation will vary within project teams. Consider running a simple one or two day course at the beginning of a major project to get everyone at the same level of understanding; and
- Assuming that customers/sponsors have distributed simulation, DIS and/or HLA knowledge. (I have been told to implement DIS over the Internet and on a large non-government organization business critical WAN. I have been told that the simulation software doesn't work properly but the 2 million polygon model the customer imported to use in it worked fine in the CAD program just this morning.) There are no easy answers to customer knowledge transfer. Presentation of a copy of this book as a gift to those people might be useful. For those receiving this book as a gift, it is because….er, the person giving it thought that you could share your extensive experience with the Author as a case study in future editions.

Data Issues

There are various common issues relating to data that may appear when implementing a distributed simulation. Some of these are:

- Limited access to internal simulation data. Before data can be transferred from one model or simulation to another, such as position data, the data must be accessed. Access can be gained using an Application Programming Interface (API), dynamic link libraries (DLL), or other mechanisms. Some simulation systems are not able to provide access to these internal data structures for easy conversion into DIS or HLA environments. This can be a problem when attempting to integrate gaming technology into traditional simulation environments for example;

- Data types. The data types that are supported in applications can be very different between similar simulations. For example, a simulator may not support long, real, or integer types. Some form of middleware may be required to map different data types for compatibility resolution;

- Attribute name issues. There are no specific standards for naming attributes. A developer may choose to call a detonation event "explosion", while another might call theirs "blast". A table may be created to map explosion to blast and vice versa in order to translate values between simulators;

- Coordinate conversion. Also refer to the Terrain chapter in this book. Coordinate conversions are necessary between different systems and datum's. A single system should be agreed to and all non-conforming simulators will need to provide a conversion mechanism in order for it to interoperate correctly with other simulators;

- Failure to replicate reality. The models, systems and processes used may not effectively replicate reality adequately to produce useable results. (Review the chapter on VV&A.). Common issues include bullets and artillery shrapnel that do not pass through thin wood, human avatars that never get tired and so on;

- Network Time Management. Problems will occur if time is not consistent throughout the distributed simulation infrastructure. Data delivery will be affected if systems on the network believe that data delivered to them was delivered late and thus should be discarded. Network time should be synchronized using a centralized Network Time Server wherever possible; and

- Does the software perform as advertised? Some software unfortunately does not and can crash if out-of-bounds data is received. A couple of examples I have come across include a simulator crashing when receiving anything but Entity State PDU's, another crashed when receiving electromagnetic emission PDUs. Both advertised that they were "IEEE 1516 compliant".

Configuration Issues

One of the more frustrating troubleshooting exercises faced when implementing a distributed simulation environment is sorting out the various configuration files and ensuring that everything is communicating properly. The most common issues are:

- FDD file mismatches. Although there is supposed to be only one FDD file per federation, sometimes different FDD files or versions can be mistakenly used. This is the FOM data, so using the wrong FDD file, means that the wrong FOM is being used;
- RID file. There are a couple of common mistakes with RID files:
    - Using the default RID RTI file without editing it for use within the specific distributed simulation network environment. (The default RID file will contain sample data that is supposed to be edited by the RTI user to update the IP addresses used etc.);
    - Re-using an older RID file from another exercise that contains invalid settings; and
    - Watch out for typos with the Federation name contained in the file. If it isn't correct and federates are looking for a specific name, they cannot join the federation.
- DIS simulator and Federate configuration files. The most common types of files are listed under "Federation Configuration Files" from page 108. Common issues are:
    - Typos for federation or exercise names;
    - Wrong IP addresses;
    - DIS Version used is not supported by other simulators in exercise;
    - Different terrain coordinate systems;
    - Terrain origin point is wrong; and
    - Entity enumerations are mismatched, or wrong.

Forgetting Logistics

OK, so this is more of an exercise and scenario design issue, but something that is overlooked in 99% of distributed simulation events (and exercises in general) is logistics. There are logistics PDUs that can be utilized in both DIS and HLA. This includes service requests, resupply and repair. Also remember that it will take time for these activities to be completed. Many exercises are rushed through and deemed successful even though on several occasions during execution all vehicles are magically refueled, or 10,000 tonnes of supplies are somehow flown-in from a different country and distributed to refugees in a few minutes or hours in order to expediently complete a mission. The fact is that until you have actually planned and implemented the logistics supporting the operation you are exercising, you will not appreciate how contingent those logistics are to the success or failure of your operation.

"My logisticians are a humorless lot ... they know if my campaign fails, they are the first ones I will slay."
- Alexander the Great

Consider using a SAF/CGF application for logistics to ensure that the supply chain is fully simulated. A resupply request PDU can be sent from the simulator to the SAF/CGF for processing and fulfillment. The application will determine if the supply request can be processed from existing stores and then virtually send the supplies by road, rail or air to the requesting organization.

Documentation

Some project documentation issues to be aware of are:

- For geographically distributed teams, consider an online repository such as Microsoft SharePoint or Microsoft Groove Office to store key project documents. In some cases, there will be issues of access for some personnel, such as military staff, or sub-contractors behind firewalls. In such cases, they may need external internet access in order to participate in these shared spaces;

- It may be a good idea to include a technical writer on the project team, particularly if the project will be creating a new simulation environment that will be re-used after the project is complete. A technical writer will be able to produce technical, operator and maintenance manuals and will free up development staff to concentrate on their area of expertise. It is a rare developer that is also good at producing technical manuals; and

- It is always a good idea to spend some time documenting lessons learned <u>during</u> the project, not afterwards. Schedule some time each week to discuss these and ask the team to send the project manager a quick email outlining the lesson learned as they are discovered. A format can be arranged to capture the data before starting and potentially a SharePoint or other web-based database could be used. Suggested fields are;
    - o   Unique identifier for the lesson learned;
    - o   Title;
    - o   Key words;
    - o   Submission Details;
        - ▪   Date submitted;
        - ▪   Lesson identified by;
        - ▪   Organization;
        - ▪   Contact Details;
    - o   Project/Task;
    - o   Lesson/s learned;
    - o   Recommendation (if required); and
    - o   Additional comments/information/links.

Project Issues

There are a myriad of issues that will regularly follow projects around. Simulation projects are not immune from these. Some common issues are:

- Perception that distributed simulation is an easy job. "This simulator is DIS compatible and that simulator is as well. Just hook it up and it will all work.";

- Reporting what the client wants to hear rather than what the simulation results are. There are times when things go horribly wrong, or results are completely unexpected. The simulation environment could fail, or there may be problems with some aspects that are caused by lack of oversight, human error, or causes outside of your control. Be open and forthright and tell it like it is. Don't candy-coat the results, at the same time there may be ways to present the results so that the landing will be cushioned. (I still have lots to learn in this area!);

- Lack of understanding of output analysis results. When we use data logging software in our distributed simulation environment, there are a lot of ways to present the data in a fashion that makes sense to technical and non-technical project sponsors. It is in your best interest to present output analysis results in a human-readable format that makes sense;

- Bang for buck. It is human nature that the more money is spent on a project, the more results are expected to be seen. A simple yes/no answer after spending $1 Million on a problem is most likely going to be judged on the weight of the document that expresses the answer, than on the answer itself. The same with simulation. Effective cost-benefit analysis during the planning phase should mitigate such perceptions; and

- Find the right people to do the job. Success or failure may depend upon not just the technical expertise of the people involved, but their personality and willingness to contribute to the team. Major projects have been derailed just because of one bad hiring decision. If this occurs within your project, quick and decisive action sooner rather than later will save escalation of the issue later on.

10   Verification, Validation and Accreditation

Introduction

When we create a distributed simulation, we normally bring together a collection of models and simulations to use within the environment we are creating. How do we know however, if the model or simulation is suitable for its intended use? In other words, does it have credibility and how do we know if it does? You may have found the perfect fast-jet simulator that you want to use for your exercise, but discover that it can fly at MACH 20 and crashes into clouds. A small arms simulator can simulate all of the infantry weapons that you need for your event, but hand-gun bullets can fly out in a perfectly straight line for 10 km and cannot penetrate a sheet of paper. The bad-guys can be perfectly safe if they hide behind a bed-sheet hanging on a clothes line.

The purpose of Verification, Validation and Accreditation (VV&A) is to ensure that we develop and use correct and valid models and simulations for their intended purpose and that we have a way of providing users with enough information to determine if they can meet their needs.

This chapter will introduce concepts relating to VV&A for consideration when you plan and implement a distributed simulation environment[34]. VV&A processes are used to establish the credibility of models and simulations for their intended use. A model or simulation that is unable to be used in a particular distributed simulation may be perfect in another context. The factors that determine suitability are therefore specific to the instance of the distributed simulation environment being implemented, not the specific model or simulation by itself. The underlying theme in this chapter is that a one-size-fits-all process

---

[34] Also refer to IEEE 1516.4 2007. This is the standard titled "Recommended Practice for VV&A, an overly to the HLA FEDEP" and the DoD VV&A Recommended Practices Guide (RPG) at: http://vva.msco.mil/

cannot be specified, the approach must be tailored to the specific needs of the distributed simulation activity being undertaken.

Definitions

There are many variations in the definition of VV&A depending on the source. They will vary in semantics and language, but in most cases have the same underlying themes indicated in the definitions presented in the following pages.

Verification

1. The process of evaluating software and its associated data to determine whether the products of a given development phase satisfy the conditions imposed at the start of the phase;
2. Verification is ensuring that the product is designed to deliver all the functionalities to the customer which involve the requirements and design specifications; and
3. Verification ensures that **'YOU BUILD THE THING RIGHT'**.

Validation

1. The process of evaluating software and its associated data during or at the end of the development process to determine whether it satisfies the specified requirements and that it provides an accurate representation of the real world from the perspective of the intended uses of the model;
2. Validation ensures that the product actually meets the user's needs and the specifications were correct in the first place; and
3. Validation ensures that **'YOU BUILD THE RIGHT THING'**.

Accreditation

1. Accreditation is the process in which official certification of competency, authority or credibility is presented that a model or simulation and its associated data is acceptable for a specific purpose;
2. Accreditation indicates that the agencies certification practices are competent to test and certify third parties; and
3. Accreditation determines **'SHOULD IT BE USED?'** (..for its intended purpose).

The Importance of VV&A

The importance of VV&A, within the distributed simulation project, is related to the intended use of the model or simulation within it. An example is given below to help illustrate this point:

1. A helicopter is used in a distributed simulation to train a search and rescue pilot how to approach a ship in distress in high seas; and
2. A helicopter is used in a distributed simulation to train rear-seat observers to spot forest fires.

In both examples above, a helicopter is used, however a high-fidelity flight model (and most likely a good sea state model) will be required for the first example in order to train the pilot in a more realistic fashion. There is a high risk of lives and equipment being lost in the real world. The second example is about training the observer, therefore the flight model is not important and not really required. The helicopter model could be placed in a stationary hover position by a non-pilot, or the computer could "fly" it from point A to point B in a straight line.

Our VV&A investigation would determine that a high-fidelity (and thus, probably very expensive) flight model is required for the first example and the same flight model could be used for the second, or preferably a low-fidelity flight model (potentially low cost, or no flight model at all), could be used. The reverse situation is not tenable because our intended use dictates to us that a low-fidelity flight model would not meet the intended purpose of the distributed simulation.

This brings us to the potential budget implications of poorly implemented VV&A processes. Although not a simulation project on its own, the Mars Climate Orbiter had modeling and simulation components within the project that played a crucial part in its failure. In September 1999, the spacecraft made a small smudge in the atmosphere of Mars and burnt up because of a unit of measurement error. The contractor team responsible for the navigation thrusters in the US did not use international standard units (metric) which is what their European counterparts were using, the spacecraft missed its target altitude and couldn't maintain orbit. It also used software from the earlier Mars Global Surveyor mission and had not been adequately tested before launch. Included in the eight contributing factors of the NASA Mars Climate Orbiter Failure board[35] were the following observations:

- errors went undetected within ground-based computer models of how small thruster firings on the spacecraft were predicted and then carried out on the spacecraft during its interplanetary trip to Mars; and

---

[35] The full report can be downloaded from the following site: ftp://ftp.hq.nasa.gov/pub/pao/reports/1999/MCO_report.pdf

- the process to verify and validate certain engineering requirements and technical interfaces between some project groups, and between the project and its prime mission contractor, was inadequate.

This proved to be an expensive $327.6 million mistake with VV&A playing a leading role in the subsequent failure.

VV&A provides an understanding of the assumptions, capabilities and limitations of the models and simulations. VV&A also promotes reuse by allowing others to understand how the process has been used to determine the capability and thus credibility of the model or simulation.

V&V Process

The basic V&V activities that can be applied to a distributed simulation project are:

1. **Verification of the M&S Requirements.** Confirm that the user/sponsor requirements are correct and complete (as outlined in Step 1: Define Simulation Environment Objectives on Page 120);
2. **Develop the V&V Plan.** This plan, in concert with the project plan and accreditation plan, will identify the objectives, priorities, risks, tasks, schedule, personnel and resource requirements of the V&V endeavor;
3. **Verification of the Design.** Ensure that the design contains all necessary elements of the needed capabilities;
4. **Verification of the Implementation.** Determine through measurable and recordable means that the code is correct and implemented correctly on the hardware; and
5. **Validate the Results.** Determine the extent to which the model or simulation addresses the requirements of the intended use.

Independent Verification and Validation

Independent Verification and Validation (IV&V) means that a completely independent entity, group or body evaluates the work products generated by the team that is designing and/or executing a given project. The IV&V provider will monitor and evaluate every aspect of the project itself from inception to completion. It is assumed that the IV&V provider has the same or higher level of expertise than the team designing and implementing the product.

Examples include professional bodies that will V&V climate and weather models, government research establishments validating clinical trial results and so on.

Accreditation Process

The end result of the accreditation process is to officially certify that a model or simulation and its associated data are fit for the intended use it is being applied to. The following general steps are undertaken during the accreditation process:

1. **Develop the Accreditation Plan.** This plan, in concert with the project and V&V plans, will identify all of the information and resources needed to perform the accreditation assessment. It will list the objectives, priorities, risks, tasks, schedule, personnel and resource requirements to complete the assessment;
2. **Collect and Evaluate Accreditation Information.** In accordance with the plan, the information required to conduct the assessment is gathered and evaluated;
3. **Perform Assessment.** The fitness of the model or simulation for the specified use is assessed using all of the data collected. An accreditation report and recommendations are prepared and delivered to the User.

The accreditation process should be conducted as early as possible within the distributed simulation project. This allows the selection of suitable models and simulations as early as possible in the project and decisions on whether to discard, build or buy others that are required to be made with as much lead-time as possible.

Accreditation Results

The specific accreditation results and terminology used will vary within organizations. The suggested options are listed below[36]:

1. **Full accreditation.** The simulation produces results that are sufficiently credible to support the application;
2. **Limited or conditional accreditation.** Constraints should be placed on how the simulation can be used to support the application. These constraints should be

---

[36] These are contained within the US DoD VV&A RPG at the following website. http://vva.msco.mil/

documented with as much detail as possible to allow for informed decisions on the intended use of the model or simulation by the User.

3. **Modification of the simulation is needed.** The simulation's capabilities are insufficient to support either full or conditional accreditation; modifications and subsequent V&V are needed to correct the deficiencies;

4. **Additional information is needed.** The information obtained about the simulation is insufficient to support either full or conditional accreditation. Additional information should be generated or otherwise obtained, supplemental verification, validation and/or testing should be conducted to provide the necessary information before the accreditation decision is made; and

5. **No accreditation.** The results of the assessment show that the simulation does not adequately support the application.

Appendix A: Distributed Simulation Agreements Template

"Project/Exercise/Mission Name"

Distributed Simulation Agreements

EXAMPLE

This template is a modification of an original DoD Federation Agreements Document that has been successfully used by the Author in various distributed simulation exercises internationally.

1. Purpose

The purpose of this document is to record all the agreements between (federates/simulators) required to support simulation interoperability for _____ Project. Paragraph 56 of this document outlines the operational scenario to be implemented for this specific exercise.

This document may also serve as a template for future distributed simulation agreements between _____ and other simulators/federates or federations.

2. Document Versions and Updates

This is a living document that will be updated as additional information is gathered for the distributed simulation. Each update if this document will be labeled by an incremental version number. Corrections should be submitted to _____, email address _____, phone _____.

3. References

The following references are relevant to this document:

- A. Guidance, Rationale, and Interoperability Modalities for the Real-time Platform Reference Federation Object Model (RPR FOM), Version 2.0, DRAFT 17v3, 3 October 2003.
- B. IEEE 1516-2000 - IEEE Standard for Modelling and Simulation (M&S) High Level Architecture (HLA) - Framework and Rules provides the rules and definitions for implementing and using HLA. Its IEEE product code is SH94882.
- C. IEEE 1516.1-2000 - IEEE Standard for Modelling and Simulation (M&S) High Level Architecture (HLA) - Federate Interface Specification defines the various services provided by an HLA RTI, and contains the APIs. Its IEEE product code is SH94883.
- D. IEEE 1516.2-2000 - IEEE Standard for Modelling and Simulation (M&S) High Level Architecture (HLA) - Object Model Template (OMT) Specification defines the format used for describing object models in HLA. An object model dictates what kinds of data a particular set of HLA federates will be exchanging. The IEEE product code for this document is SH94884.
- E. IEEE 1516.3-2003 - IEEE Standard for Modelling and Simulation (M&S) High Level Architecture (HLA) – Recommended Practices Guide for Federation Development and Execution Process (FEDEP).

F.   IEEE 1278.1a-1998 IEEE standard for Distributed Interactive Simulation (DIS).

G.   SISO-REF-010-2006. Enumeration and Bit Encoded Values for use with Protocols for Distributed Interactive Simulation Applications

4. RTI and FOM

Optional. This section is only if you are using an HLA component within your distributed simulation project.

The Runtime Infrastructure (RTI) application to be used within the _____ project is _____ from _____.

The diagram below shows the intended federation/distributed simulation structure for the _____ project.

5. RTI Services

Optional. This section is only if you are using an HLA component within your distributed simulation project.

The federation shall only call the following services to initiate federation events:

1.   Federation Management
    a.   Join Federation Execution
    b.   Resign Federation Execution
        i.   When a federate resigns it can choose whether to include a directive to delete all objects for which it has delete privileges
    c.   Synchronization points TBD

      d. The use of the RTI save and restore services is not allowed. Federates will perform independent saves and restores

      e. Publish Object Class

      f. Unpublish Object Class

      g. Publish Interaction Class

      h. Unpublish Interaction Class

      i. Subscribe Object Class Attributes

      j. Unsubscribe Object Class

      k. Subscribe Interaction Class

      l. Unsubscribe Interaction Class

2. Object Management

      a. Register Object Instance

      b. Delete Object Instance

      c. Local Delete Object Instance

      d. Update Attribute Values

      e. Send Interaction.

      f. Request Attribute Value Update

      g. Provide Attribute Value Update

3. Ownership Management will not be used

4. Time Management will not be used

5. Data Distribution Management will not be used

6. Support Services

      a. All advisories will be unavailable

7. MOM Services

      a. MOM services will be unavailable

6. Simulation Management

All federates will run in real time as defined by the current ROMEO (Eastern Standard Time – EST) wall clock time. Federates recovering from a fault by reloading a past state must be able to catch up to the current ROMEO wall clock time. It need not be published by any federate as events will be accepted in Received Order (see paragraph below). Prior to joining the Federation, systems should synchronize system time with an Internet time provider such as time.windows.com for EST/ROMEO time.

7. Time of Events

All attribute updates and interactions will be accepted in Received Order and will not be time tagged. Instead, the time of the event represented by the attribute update or interaction will be considered to have occurred at the local system time at which it is received.

8. Optional Attributes and Parameters

List all optional attributes that are to be used.

9. Updates and Queries

There are four reasons for updating object parameters:

1. Value change;
2. Threshold limit exceed;
3. Heartbeats; and
4. Queries.

A particular response to an attribute value to is determined by the individual attribute. Some attributes such as damage state will be updated whenever their value changes. These are typically discrete attributes. Continuous attributes such as position are only updated after some threshold has been exceeded. The only thresholds _____ project uses are dead reckoning thresholds.

Attributes may be updated due to queries. Federates may query for attributes only if absolutely necessary. Therefore, no simulation should query for attributes until the timeout period has passed.

Do not query until 90 seconds after an object has entered delayed discovery. Don't repeat your query more often than the timeout and don't query by class. Alternatively you can eliminate delayed discovery and throw away all attributes until you get the heartbeat. A federate must stop querying once it gets it's create set for an object. A create set is the minimum set of attributes required to locally create the object. The create set is not allowed to include any optional _____project attributes. Federates should not receive any queries for attributes that they are not actually publishing (as such queries should be filtered by the RTI).

10. Identifiers

Each federation object must have a unique RTI identifier. This identifier must be specified by the application when registering the object. The application is responsible for making sure that the ID is federation unique. To do this and to allow monitoring of entities by source simulation, we are going to require that each RTI name start with the name of the simulation producing the object followed by a unique identifier:

<application name>/<your locally unique id here>[37]

For example:

----

[37] : Note that in some organizations the standard is IP Address and Application ID. Using this secondary approach an identifier would look like this: 192.168.13.55/SIM1.

PR/01

MAWS/44

(1)   \<application name\> must come from the following list of names. If your application does not have a name here please the Federation Manager to get it added. The critical factor about these names is that the first two characters are unique for each simulation. That way monitor applications can determine which simulation the entity comes from by only doing a string compare on the first two characters. Case is significant.

(2)   _____ Federation (examples below);

    (a)   **SIM1**

    (b)   **UAVSIM**

    (c)   **PREPAR3D**

    (d)   **MANPADS**

11. Coordinate Systems

All network world position representations shall use the Geocentric Coordinate System (GCC), defined as a coordinate system with origin at the centre of the earth, Z axis projected through the North Pole, X axis projecting through zero degrees latitude and zero degrees longitude, and the Y axis projecting through 90 degrees East longitude and 0 degrees latitude. Distances are measured in meters.

All network world position representations shall use the Geocentric Coordinate System (GCC), defined as a coordinate system with origin at the centre of the earth, Z axis projected through the North Pole, X axis projecting through zero degrees latitude and zero degrees longitude, and the Y axis projecting through 90 degrees East longitude and 0 degrees latitude. Distances are measured in meters.

The _____ project working terrain database is expected to have the following attributes:

Geographic Area Of Coverage: 00 deg 00'00" N to 00 deg 00'00" N and 00 deg 00'00" E to 00 deg 00'00" E

Projection: UTM

Geodetic Datum: Horizontal - WGS 84; Vertical – Mean Sea Level

12. Kinematic Attributes

The following attributes will be used to represent an object's kinematic state. These attributes will always be updated atomically even if only one requires an update.

1. Position: x, y, z (meters);
2. Velocity: x, y. z (meters per second); and
3. Orientation: yaw, pitch, roll (radians).

Acceleration and angular velocity are optional. Remember to use RelativeSpatial to express the spatial relationship between an entity and a host entity (i.e. missile to missile launcher, aircraft to aircraft carrier) or Spatial to express the relationship between the entity and the centre of the Earth. (Refer to BaseEntity Attributes)

13. SpatialStruct Attributes

Reference A, para 5.14.11 states:

RPR FOM 2.0 has changed the way that Time, Space and Position Information (TSPI) is transmitted for performance reasons. This does cause a compatibility issue with the initial release of RPR FOM 1.0, but it was felt that the performance gains warranted the transition and RPR FOM 1.0 may be modified to use the new system as well. The new system uses one variant record to store all of the TSPI and dead reckoning information into a single attribute instead of several attributes. The attributes that have been incorporated into this record are: AccelerationVector, AngularVelocityVector, DeadReckoningAlgorithm, IsFrozen, Orientation, VelocityVector and WorldLocation. The DeadReckoningAlgorithm provides the discriminator for the variant record, selecting which structure is used, determining how much information needs to be sent.

Reference A para 6.1 states:

The dead reckoning algorithm field of the spatial attribute allows the simulating federate to dictate whether and how reflecting federates perform dead-reckoning. When all reflecting federates perform dead-reckoning in the same way, they are able to share a more consistent view of the state of the virtual world.

14. Dead Reckoning

To reduce the rate at which kinematic data between federates is updated, dead reckoning shall be used. Each federate shall maintain a dead reckoning position model for entities.

This model shall be used to update the position of remote entities when performing calculations with the entity's position data. For its own objects the federate will periodically compare the true position with the dead reckoned position and if the errors exceed the thresholds defined here, all kinematic attributes shall be updated. All federates shall support a simple first order dead reckoning algorithm for position defined by

$$\mathbf{p}(t+dt) = \mathbf{p}(t) + \mathbf{v}(t)*t$$

This algorithm is called algorithm DRM_FPW or #2 in DIS terms. No dead reckoning of the remaining kinematic attributes will be used.

15. Update Thresholds

An entity's kinematic attributes shall be updated once the error between their dead reckoned position and their true position exceeds

1. Position, error along any axis exceeds 1.0 meter along each dimension (see Entity Coordinates below for origin), and
2. Orientation, error around any axis exceeds 15 degrees.

Only entities will be updated if DR thresholds are exceeded. All other objects such as aggregates will only be updated on heartbeats and change events.

16. Entity Coordinates

The DIS Standard defines the position of an entity as the position of its centre of mass. While this is natural for aircraft it causes extra computation for ground and surface entities. To save that computation the meaning of a vehicle's position and orientation shall be:

1. For aircraft the z origin of their coordinate systems shall be at the centre of mass of the aircraft;
2. For ground entities the z origin of their coordinate systems shall be located at the bottom of the object; and
3. For surface vessels the z origin of their coordinate systems shall be at the nominal waterline of the entity.

Angular orientation shall be represented by three angles (Euler Angles) defined as follows. All rotations should be done in order presented below:

1. yaw - rotate around vertical axis through the vehicle. Positive rotation is clockwise when looking down at the vehicle.
2. pitch - rotate around axis through the width of the vehicle. Positive rotation is clockwise when looking out the right side of the vehicle.

3. roll - rotate around axis through the length of the vehicle. Positive rotation is clockwise looking out the front of the vehicle.

17. Ground Clamping

Best efforts by federate developers should be made to reduce the requirement for ground clamping. If ground clamping is required, this will reduce performance of the target federate, particularly when large numbers of entities enter the viewport. It is assumed that _____ project efforts being made to produce consistent terrain databases for all of the federates will eliminate the need for ground clamping, however it is recognized that there may be limitations in some systems. Please identify ground clamping requirements to the author of this document ASAP for impact analysis.

18. User Defined Tags

Time tags in the user defined tag of every Update Attributes Value and Send Interactions call will be optional.

19. Data Type Representation

For simple data types use those provided by the OMT with the exception of "any" which should not be used.

20. Endianess

Big endian byte ordering will be used for attribute and parameter types on the network.

21. Alignment and Padding

All data types will be aligned on natural boundaries, with explicit padding filling in any gaps. Thus byte long data elements should lie on byte boundaries, and 8 byte data elements should start on addresses that are a multiple of 8 bytes. Strings are considered an array of 1-byte elements and thus can occur at any byte address. For more detail refer to the GRIM for the RPR FOM (Reference A).

22. Transport Mechanisms

Object Class Attribute updates will be delivered using reliable. Interactions will be delivered using best effort.

23. Timeouts

Objects will be timed out after they have not been heard from for 90 seconds.

24. Entity Representations

All simulations shall publish entity resolution objects for all their owned forces. All simulations shall output the unit hierarchies for their forces using aggregate state objects. These aggregate representations will be used by simulation displays to show aggregated situation displays with a capability for drill down to entity level. Platform representations shall not publish any articulations.

25. Combat Interactions

All combat interactions on the primary federation shall be resolved on an individual entity and detonation basis. However, detonations can use the burst parameter to indicate multiple rounds. For engagement of flying air entities, only direct fire detonations shall be used. Flying air vehicle may ignore indirect fire munitions.

26. Entity Enumerations

All legal entities and munitions are provided in the ___project enumerations list below.

Blue Forces

Serial	Entity Type	Total Number Required	DIS Entity Number	Notes
1	LAV III	5	1:1:39:0:5:21	• Appended simulators
2	Infantry	30	3:1:39:1:103	• VBS
3	…			•
4	…			•

Red Forces

Serial	Entity Type	Total Number Required	DIS Entity Number	Notes
1	Infantry	10	3:1:222:1:103	• JSAF
2	AFV	2	1:1:222:2:4:6	• VBS – (BRDM2)
3	…			•
4	…			•

Civilian

Serial	Entity Type	Total Number Required	DIS Entity Number	Notes
1				•
2				•
3				•

4	...			•

Munitions

Serial	Entity Type	Total Number Required	DIS Entity Number	Notes
1	7.62 mm MG Tracer		2:8:39:2:2:1:1	•
2				•
3	...			•

27. Aggregate Enumerations

Aggregate enumerations will have the same structure as entity enumerations, but will make use of the following enumerations. Aggregates will only be used for Land and Air units. Surface, Subsurface, and Space entities will not generate aggregates.

1. KIND
   a. Other
   b. Military Hierarchy
   c. Common Type
   d. Common Mission
   e. Similar Capabilities
   f. Common Location
2. DOMAIN - Same as for entities
3. COUNTRY - Same as for entities
4. CATEGORY
   a. Other
   b. IndividualVehicle
   c. Element
   d. Platoon
   e. Battery
   f. Company
   g. Battalion
   h. Regiment
   i. Brigade
   j. Division
   k. Corps
   l. IndividualAircraft
   m. Flight
5. SUBCATEGORY

      a.   Other
      b.   CavalryTroop
      c.   Armor
      d.   Infantry
      e.   MechanizedInfantry
      f.   Cavalry
      g.   ArmoredCavalry
      h.   Artillery
      i.   SelfPropelledArtillery
      j.   CloseAirSupport
      k.   Engineer
      l.   AirDefenseArtillery
      m.   AntiTank
      n.   AviationFixedWing
      o.   AviationRotaryWing
      p.   AttackHelicopter
      q.   AirCavalry
      r.   ArmorHeavyTaskForce
      s.   MotorizedRifle
      t.   MechanizedHeavyTaskForce
      u.   CommandPost
      v.   CEWI
      w.   TankOnly
      x.   AirForce
      y.   Bomber
      z.   Fighter

6. SPECIFIC

      a.   NoHeadquarters
      b.   ContainsHeadquarters

28. Countermeasures

The GMS Federation will represent the following types of countermeasures:

1. Concealment; and
2. Decoys –Chaff (CMDS on Utility Helo).

28.1. Concealment

Concealment will be represented in this project by means of the IsConcealed attribute of the PhysicalEntity class. This Boolean is to be set when the entity enters a cave, building, or a vehicle. No sensor should detect an entity that has its IsConcealed bit set. UAV models should not display concealed entities.

28.2 Decoys – Chaff

To be determined.

29. Objects and Interactions

This section explains any changes or extensions to the FOM being used. In this case, it is the RPR-FOM v2.0 draft 17. Examples of these are provided in the following sections. (Not all data is presented in these examples, it is for illustration purposes.)

30. Object Classes

Mission Object Class Structure			
Class 1	**Class 2**	**Class 3**	**Class 4**
ActivSonarBeam			
BaseEntity	AggregateEntity		
	EnvironmentalEntity		
	PhysicalEntity	Platform	Aircraft
			Ground Vehicle
		Lifeform	Human
			Non-Human
		Expendables	
		Munition	
		Radio	
		Sensor	
		Supplies	
EmbeddedSystem	EmitterSystem		
	IFF	NATOIFF	NatoIFFInterrogator
			NATOIFFTransponder
EmitterBeam			
	RadarBeam		
EnvironmentObject	AreaObject	MineFieldObject	
		OtherAreaObject	

EnvironmentProcess			

31. The BaseEntity Class

The BaseEntity class provides the attributes necessary to describe the position and motion of an independent object in the simulated world.

Attribute Name	DIS PDU	DIS Field	IEEE 1278 Reference	Definition
Entity Identifier	Entity State	Entity ID	1995:5.3.3.1.b	Identifies the site, application, and entity number of this object instance. It is used for group addressing in the SIMAN interactions.
EntityType	Entity State	Entity Type	1995:5.3.3.1.e	Kind, Country, Domain, Category, Subcategory, Specific, and Extra fields of the DIS Entity Type.
IsPartOf	IsPartOf	Originating Entity, Relationship, Named Location	1998:5.3.9.4.b, 5.3.9.4.d, 5.3.9.4.f,	Used to indicate that there is a spatial relationship between this entity and a host entity, i.e., one entity is "part of" another
RelativeSpatial	Entity State, Is Part Of	Dead reckoning Alg., Position, Velocity, Acceleration, Orientation, Angular Velocity	1995:5.3.3.1.g, 5.3.3.1.h, 5.3.3.1.i , 5.3.3.1.k.1, 5.3.3.1.k.4, 5.3.3.1.k.3	Used to express the spatial relationship between the entity and a host entity. Used in addition to the normal spatial attribute which describes absolute location.
Spatial	Entity State	Dead reckoning Alg., Position, Velocity, Acceleration, Orientation, Angular Velocity, Is Frozen	1995:5.3.3.1.g, 5.3.3.1.h, 5.3.3.1.i , 5.3.3.1.k.1, 5.3.3.1.k.4, 5.3.3.1.k.3	Used to express the spatial relationship between the entity and the center of the Earth.

32. The Aggregate Class

The Aggregate class allows the federation to determine where enemy and friendly units are without being overwhelmed by processing all the individual entities. Every non-neutral land unit should be represented by an aggregate and every aircraft should be represented by an aircraft aggregate. If a unit's HQ element consists of more than 4 entities than there should be an HQ aggregate for that unit as one of the unit's subordinates.

Required Aggregate Attributes		
ForceIdentifier	ForceIdentifierEnum8	Other, Friendly, Opposing, Neutral
Marking	MarkingStruct	11 character unit identification string
aggregate_state	Aggregate_Status_Enum32	Indicates how the unit is disaggregated Other, Aggregated, Disaggregated, Fully_disaggregated, Pseudo_disaggregated, Partially_disaggregated.
aggregate_formation	Aggregate_Formation_Enum32	Other, Assembly, Vee, Wedge, Line, Column
agg_ids_struct	RTIObjectIDStruct	Length and RTI IDs of all aggregate subordinates (see details below)
ent_ids	RTIObjectIDStruct	Length and RTI IDs for entity subordinates not in aggregate subordinates (see details below).
detached_ent_ids	RTIObjectIDStruct	Length and RTI IDs of entity subordinates not considered in COM and bounds calculations (see details below)
aggregate_extent	bounding_region	box around the aggregate: x,y,z

Aggregate Attribute Update Requirements			
ForceIdentifier	X		
Marking	X		
aggregate_state	X		
aggregate_formation	X		
agg_ids_struct	X		
ent_ids	X		
detached_ent_ids	X		
aggregate_extent	X		

33. The PhysicalEntity Class

The base class for discrete platforms in the mission. No entity will be published directly into the PhysicalEntity Class.

Required PhysicalEntity Attributes		
Attribute Name	Data Type	Use
DamageState	DamageStatusEnum32	NoDamage, SlightDamage, ModerateDamage, Destroyed
ForceIdentifier	ForceIdentifierEnum8	Other, Friendly, Opposing, Neutral
Marking	MarkingStruct	11 character entity identification string
FirePowerDisabled	boolean	Used to indicate a fire power kill on main weapon
Immobilized	boolean	Used to indicate a mobility kill
CamouflageType	CamouflageEnum32	NoCamo, Camo1, Camo2, Camo3
IsConcealed	boolean	Set if entity is inside a cave, building, or vehicle where it is difficult to detect
TrailingEffectsCode	TrailingEffectsCodeEnum32	NoTrail, SmallTrail, MediumTrail, LargeTrail, only required for munitions

PhysicalEntity Attribute Update Requirements			
Attribute Name	Heartbeat	Threshold Exception	ValueChange
DamageState	X		X
ForceIdentifier	X		N/A
Marking	X		N/A
FirePowerDisabled	X		X
Immobilized	X		X
CamouflageType	X		X
IsConcealed	X		X
TrailingEffectsCode	X		X

Optional PhysicalEntity Attributes	
Attribute Name	Default Value
AlternateEntityType	EntityType
EngineSmokeOn	FALSE
FlamesPresent	FALSE
HasAmmunitionSupplyCap	FALSE

HasFuelSupplyCap	FALSE
HasRepairCap	FALSE
HasRecoveryCap	FALSE
PowerPlantOn	FALSE
SmokePlumePresent	FALSE
TentDeployed	FALSE

34. The Munition Class

This class is a subclass of the PhysicalEntity class. It is used to represent munitions which are flown out as entities. All entities with

$$EntityTypeStruct.EntityKind = munition = 2$$

will be published to this class.

Optional Munition Attributes	
Attribute Name	DefaultValue
LauncherFlashPresent	FALSE

35. The Platform Class

The Platform class is a subclass of PhysicalEntity, which provides for a variety of appearance attributes for entities. All of these attributes are optional and default to false or NotApplicable. Federates are not required to publish these attributes or respond to their presence on an entity. No entities will be published directly to this class.

Optional Platform Attributes	
Attribute Name	DefaultValue
AfterburnerOn	FALSE
AntiCollisionLightsOn	FALSE
BlackOutBrakeLightsOn	FALSE
BlackOutLightsOn	FALSE
BrakeLightsOn	FALSE
FormationLightsOn	FALSE
HatchState	N/A
HeadlightsOn	FALSE
InteriorLightsOn	FALSE
LandingLightsOn	FALSE
LauncherRaised	FALSE
NavigationLightsOn	FALSE
RampDeployed	FALSE
RunningLightsOn	FALSE

SpotLightsOn	FALSE
TailLightsOn	FALSE

36. The Aircraft Class

Subclass of Platform class for the purposes of DM filtering. No additional attributes. All entities with

$$EntityTypeStruct.EntityKind = Platform = 1; and$$

$$EntityTypeStruct.Domain = Air = 2.$$

should be published to this class.

37. The GroundVehicle Class

Subclass of the Platform class for the purpose of DM filtering. No additional attributes. All entities with

$$EntityTypeStruct.EntityType = Platform = 1; and$$

$$EntityTypeStruct.Domain = Land = 1$$

should be published to this class, with the exception of those published to the SPArtillery and AirDefense classes below.

38-42. Reserved

(These are additional class descriptions as required.)

43. Interactions

The following interactions will be used for this exercise:

Core Interactions	
Interaction 1	**Interaction 2**
MunitionDetonation	

WeaponFire	

44. The MunitionDetonation Interaction

This interaction is for representing engagements between simulation forces. It represents both direct fire and indirect fire. The DetonationResultCode values of EntityImpact", "EntityProximateDetonation", "GroundImpact" and "GroundProximateDetonation" shall be used for direct fire engagments, with the first value indicating a direct hit, the second indicating a near hit, which may or may not cause damage, and the last two indicating a miss, which will not cause damage.

The DetonationResultCode value of "Detonation" shall be used for indirect fire engagements. For direct fire detonations, damage should be computed using the RelativeDetonationLocation (target relative coordinates). For indirect fire detonations, damage should be computed using the DetonationLocation (world coordinates).

When firing at aircraft it is required that direct fire be used. That is, the DetonationResultCode shall be one of the direct fire values and that the TargetObjectIdentifier shall specify the target entity and the RelativeDetonationLocation shall give the location of the impact in the coordinates of the target.

Required MunitionDetonation Parameters		
Parameter Name	Data Type	Use
DetonationLocation	WorldLocationStruct	Location in world coordinates.
EventIdentifier	EventIdentifierStruct	ID generated by firer to associate firing and detonation.
FuseType	FusetypeEnum16	Specified by enumeration.
MunitionType	EntityTypeStruct	Kind, Country, Domain, Category, Subcategory, Specific, Extra
WarheadType	WarheadTypeEnum16	Specified by enumeration.
DetonationResultCode	DetonationResultCodeEnum8	Type of detonation (direct/indirect) and hit/miss.
QuantityFired	unsigned short	Quantity of rounds fired in a burst.

Optional MunitionDetonation Parameters		
Parameter Name	Data Type	Use
FiringObjectIdentifier	empty	Required for direct fire.

TargetObjectIdentifier	empty	Required for direct fire.
RelativeDetonationLocation	empty	Required for direct fire.
FinalVelocityVector	0,0,0	none
MunitionObjectIdentifier	empty	none
RateOfFire	1	none

45. The WeaponFire Interaction

This interaction is used to announce whenever a weapon is fired. This interaction is required for missile launches including the MANPAD used in the scenario.

Required WeaponFire Parameters		
Parameter Name	Data Type	Use
EventIdentifier	EventIdentifierStruct	ID generated by firer to associate firing and detonation.
FiringLocation	WorldLocationStruct	Launch location.
FiringObjectIdentifier	RTIObjectIDStruct	ID of issuer of interaction.
FuseType	FusetypeEnum16	Specified by enumeration.
InitialVelocityVector	VelocityVectorStruct	Velocity of munition when externally visible.
MunitionType	EntityTypeStruct	Kind, Country, Domain, Category, Subcategory, Specific, Extra
WarheadType	WarheadTypeEnum10	Specified by enumeration.

46. Operational Scenario

46.1 Distributed Simulation Training Demonstration

To show how a simulation system in a network configuration can support distributed training in a typical training scenario.

The training scenario will be based upon the following lesson plan:

46.1.1 LessonPlan001

(1)   Performance. Perform casualty evacuation (CASEVAC) with UAV Support and MANPADS threat detection and evasion.

(2)   Conditions:

(a)   Given:

(i)   Tactical helicopter simulator and crew;

(ii)   Medium lift helicopter simulator and crew;

(iii)   Tactical mission;

(iv)   Either front seat;

(v)   Individual protective equipment;

(vi)   Mission planning information;

(vii)   Aircraft performance card;

(viii)   Tactical Helicopter Checklist;

(ix)   Tactical Helicopter Flight Manual;

(x)   Medium lift Helicopter Checklist;

(xi)   Medium lift Helicopter Flight Manual;

(xii)   VFR flight information publications and maps;

(xiii)   Prepared and unprepared landing areas in urban environment;

(xiv)   Confined areas;

(xv)   Missile threats;

(xvi)   Serviceable simulated Missile Approach Warning System;

(xvii)   Serviceable simulated UAV with functioning Video link;

(xviii)   Army radio net (C2); and

(xix)   Supervision.

(b)   Denied: assistance with individual duties; and

(c)   Environmental:

     (i)   Weather clear, visibility within limits of Tactical Helicopter IG;

     (ii)   Day;

     (iii)   Tactical conditions; and

(iv)   Psychological stress.

(3)   Standard. In accordance with specified references and established procedures, procedures, with due regard for safety and airmanship, student will perform CASEVAC with UAV Support.

(4)   Teaching Points.

    (a)   CASEVAC with UAV Support procedures;

    (b)   MAWS Mission Kit Operation procedures;

    (c)   Remote Video Display & Data link Mission Kit Operation procedures; and

    (d)   Tactical Evasive Manoeuvres (for MANPADS threat).

(5)   Time.

    (a)   1 X 30 min GLP; and

    (b)   1 X 1.5 hrs Tactical Helicopter LP.

(6)   Method. Lecture/demo/performance.

(7)   Substantiation. To allow the trainee to learn by doing.

(8)   Reference. TBD

(9)   Training Aids

    (a)   Digital projector;

    (b)   Stealth Viewer for data replay;

    (c)   White board; and

    (d)   Model aircraft.

(10)   Learning Aids. Nil.

46.2 Dates

Week of 9 August 2012 (TBC).

46.3 Mission Requirements

- 2 x Tactical Helicopter simulator;

- 2 x Medium lift Helicopter simulator;

- UAV Simulator;

- Data link Model;

- Missile Threats;

- CGF as Opposing Forces;

- Data Collection Federate;

- Aircrew required to support the mission (1 crew for each Tactical and Medium lift Helicopter simulator, Instructor & Student); and

- UAV operators to support the mission.

46.4 Limitations

- Only one missile at a time will be flown out, all other missiles will be CGF entities; and

- Network must be functional and minimum bandwidth available is 2Mbps download, 250Kbps upload.

46.5 Scenario

Describe the high-level scenario here, along with maps and diagrams as required. The detailed scenario, along with the Master Sequence of Events List will also be broken out into separate documents to be distributed to the operations and role-playing staff.

Appendix B: Resources and Links

Open Source Simulation Software

Delta3D: www.delta3D.org

OpenEaagles: www.openeaagles.org

CIGI: cigi.sourceforge.net

OpenDIS: open-dis.sourceforge.net/Open-DIS.html

Portico HLA: www.porticoproject.org

OpenHLA: sourceforge.net/projects/ohla/

OpenCascade: www.opencascade.org

OpenSim: opensimulator.org

Orbiter Space Simulator: orbit.medphys.ucl.ac.uk/

FlightGear: www.flightgear.org

Open Source 3D Modeling Tools

Blender: www.blender.org

Wings3D: www.wings3d.com

Open Source Image Editing Software

GIMP: www.gimp.org

Paint.NET: paint.net

Open Source Physics Engines

Bullet: bulletphysics.org

Open Dynamics Engine: www.ode.org

Box2D: box2d.org

Open Source Miscellaneous

JSBSim (Flight Dynamics Modeling): jbsim.sourceforge.net

The Paparazzi Project (Autopilot): paparazzi.enac.fr

Physics Abstraction Layer (PAL): www.adrianboeing.com/pal/index.html

Civilian Simulation Organizations

Simulation Interoperability Standards Organization (SISO): www.sisostds.org

National Center for Simulation (US): www.simulationinformation.com

International Training and Simulation Alliance (ITSA): itsalliance.org

Society for Modeling and Simulation International (SCS): www.scs.org

National Training and Simulation Association (NTSA) (US): www.trainingsystems.org

Federation of European Simulation Societies (EuroSim): www.eurosim.info

Modelling and Simulation Society of Australia and New Zealand (MSSANZ): mssanz.org.au

Simulation Austalia: www.siaa.asn.au

Scandinavian Simulation Society: www.scansims.org

Military Simulation Organizations

US Modeling and Simulation Coordination Office (MSCO – formally known as the Defense Modeling and Simulation Office (DMSO)): www.msco.mil

US Army Modeling and Simulation Office (AMSO): www.ms.army.mil

US Air Force Agency for Modeling and Simulation (AFAMS): www.afams.af.mil

US Navy Modeling and Simulation Office (NMSO): nmso.navy.mil

Canadian Forces Synthetic Environment Coordination Office (SECO): www.cfd-cdf.forces.gc.ca

NATO Research and Technology Organization (RTO): www.rta.nato.int

Australian Defence Simulation Office (ADSO): www.defence.gov.au/capability/ADSO/

Annual Training and Simulation Conferences

Interservice/Industry Training, Simulation and Education Conference (I/ITSEC): www.iitsec.org

International Training and Education Conference (ITEC): www.itec.co.uk

SpringSim: www.scs.org/springsim

SummerSim: www.scs.org/summersim

SimTecT (Australia): www.simtect.com.au

I3M: International Mediterranean and Latin American Modelling Multiconference: www.msc-les.org

Appendix C: Abbreviations

A

AI   Artificial Intelligence

C

CAD   Computer-Aided Design
CAD/CAM   Computer Aided Design/Computer Aided Manufacturing
CBI   Computer Based Instruction
CBL   Computer Based Learning
CBT   Computer Based Training
CGF   Computer Generated Forces
CONOPS   Concept of Operations
CORBA   Common Object Request Broker Architecture
COTS   Commercial Off The Shelf

D

DET   Dynamic Environment and Terrain
DID   Data Item Description
DIS   Distributed Interactive Simulations
DL   Data Link
DME   Distributed Management Environment
DMSO   Defense Modeling and Simulation Office
DNS   Domain Name System
DOF   Degrees of Freedom
DTED   Digital Terrain Elevation Data

F

FDD   FOM Document Data
FED   Federation Execution Data
FEDEP   Federation Development and Execution Process
FOM   Federation Object Model

G

GEOREF   Geographic Reference
GOTS   Government-Off-the-Shelf
GPS   Global Positioning System

H

HLA	High-Level Architecture
HMD	Helmet Mounted Display
HMI	Human-Machine Interface
HW/SWIL	Hardware/Software-In-The-Loop

I

I/O	Input/Output
IEEE	Institute of Electrical and Electronic Engineers
IFOR	Intelligent Forces
IOC	Initial Operational Capability
IP	Internet Protocol
IS	Information System
ISDN	Integrated Services Digital Network
ISEE	Integrated Software Engineering Environment

J

JSAF	Joint Semi Automated Forces

K

kbps	Kilobits per second
KBS/DBMS	Knowledge Based Systems/Data Base Management System
kHz	Kilohertz
KI	Knowledge Integration
KOPS	Thousands of Operations Per Second
KPP	Key Performance Parameter
KRS	Knowledge Retrieval System

L

LAN	Local Area Network
LCD	Liquid Crystal Display
LED	Light-Emitting Diode
LOC	Lines of Code
LOE	Level of Effort
LRU	Line Replaceable Unit
LSB	Least Significant Bit

M

M&S	Modeling and Simulation
Mbps	Megabits per second
MCBF	Mean Cycles Between Failures
MFS	Manned Flight Simulator
MHz	Megahertz

MIL	Man-in-the-loop
MIPS	Millions of Instructions Per Second
MLS	Multi-Level Security
MOBA	Military Operations in Built-Up Areas
MOBACS	Military Operations in Built-Up Areas Combat Simulation
MOM	Management Object Model
MPDU	Message Protocol Data Unit
MSEL	Master Sequence of Events List
MSL	Mean Sea Level
MTBCF	Mean Time Between Critical Failure
MTBF	Mean Time Between Failure
MTBR	Mean Time Between Repair

N

NETOPS	Network Operations
NETWARS	Network Warfare Simulation
NFS	Network File Server
NGO	Non-Government Organization
NIC	Network Information Center
NIDR	Network Information Discover and Retrieval
NUI	Network User Interface
NVE	Night Vision Equipment
NVG	Night Vision Goggles

O

OBJ	Object
OCI	Organizational Conflict of Interest
ODBMS	Object-Oriented Data Base Management System
ODP	Open Distributed Processing
OLE	Object Linking and Embedding
OM	Object Model
OMDD	Object Model Data Dictionary
OMDT	Object Model Development Tool
OML	Object Model Library
OMT	Object Model Template
ONC	Open Network Computing
OO	Object-Oriented
OOD	Object-Oriented Design
OODA	Object-Oriented Design with Assemblies
OODA	Observation, Orientation, Decision, Action
OODB	Object-Oriented Data Base
OODBMS	Object-Oriented Database Management System
OOM	Object-Oriented Modeling
OOTW	Operations Other Than War
ORB	Object Request Broker
ORD	Operational Requirements Document
OS	Operating System
OSE	Open System Environment
OSF	Open Software Foundation
OSI	Open Systems Interconnection
OSS	Operations Support System

P

PC	Personal computer
PCB	Printed Circuit Board
PCIS	Portable Common Interface Set
PCM	Pulse Code Modulation
PDU	Protocol Data Unit
PID	Protocol Identifier Data
PK	Probability of Kill
PKI	Public Key Infrastructure
PM	Program Manager
PPTP	Point-to-Point Tunnelling Protocol
PRN	Packet Radio Network
PVD	Plain/Plan View Display

Q

QA	Quality Assurance
QC	Quality Control
QDE	Quality Data Evaluation
QDR	Quality Deficiency Report
QoS	Quality of Service

R

R-T	Real-Time
RAM	Random Access Memory
RDA	Remote Database Access
RDB	Relational Database
RDBMS	Relational Data Base Management System
REA	Remote Entity Approximation
RF	Radio Frequency
RFI	Request for Information
RFP	Request for Proposals
RFS	Remote File Sharing
RFSS	Radio Frequency Simulation System
RGS	Remote Ground Station
RID	RTI Initialization Data
RIP	Routing Information Protocol
RISC	Reduced Instruction Set Computer
RLF	Reuse Library Framework
ROM	Read Only Memory
ROM	Rough Order of Magnitude
ROV	Range of View
ROV	Remotely Operated Vehicle
ROW	Rest of the World
RTCS	Real Time Clock System
RTF	Rich Text Format
RTI	Runtime Infrastructure
RTIC	Real-Time Information In the Cockpit
RTOS	Real Time Operating System
RTV	Real Time Video
RWM	Read-Write Memory

S

S/W	Software
SA	Situational Awareness
SAF	Semi-Automated Forces
SCM	Software Configuration Management
SCORM	Sharable Content Object Reference Model
SE	Synthetic Environment
SEI	Software Engineering Institute
SEM	Spherical Earth Model
SF	Synthetic Forces
SIMNET	Simulation Network
SMART	Simulation & Modeling for Acquisition, Requirements and Training
SOL	Simulation Oriented Language
SOM	Simulation Object Model
SoS	System-of-Systems
SOW	Statement of Work
SQL	Structured Query Language
SRR	System or Software Readiness Review
SRS	System or Software Requirements Specification
SSP	Simulation Support Plan
SSR	Software Specification Review
SWCI	Software Configuration Item
SYNC	Synchronous

T

T&E	Test and Evaluation
TACSIM	Tactical Simulation
TCP	Transmission Control Protocol
TCP/IP	Transmission Control Protocol/Internet Protocol
TDL	Tactical Data Link
TDM	Time Division Multiplexer
TES	Tactical Engagement Simulation
TF	Task Force
TLSP	Transport Layer Security Protocol
TRM	Technical Reference Model
TUAV	Tactical Unmanned Aerial Vehicle

U

UAV	Unmanned Aerial Vehicles
UHF	Ultra High Frequency
UN	United Nations
UT	Universal Time
UTM	Universal Transverse Mercator
UW	Unconventional Warfare

V

VHF	Very High Frequency
VHO	Very High Orbit
VHSIC	Very High Speed Integrated Circuit

VMS	Vertical motion simulator
VMU	Voice Message Unit
VR	Virtual Reality
VSWR	Voltage Standing Wave Ratio
V&V	Verification and Validation
VV&A	Verification, Validation and Accreditation
VV&C	Verification, Validation and Certification
VSAT	Very Small Aperture Terminal

W

WAN	Wide Area Network
WGS 84	World Geodetic System 1984

Z

ZULU	Greenwich Meantime

Index

M

N

O

P

Q

R

S

CPSIA information can be obtained
at www.ICGtesting.com
Printed in the USA
FSOW04n2042110716
22631FS